REALLY, YOU'VE DONE ENOUGH

REALLY,
YOU'VE
DONE
ENOUGH

A PARENTS' GUIDE TO STOP PARENTING THEIR ADULT CHILD WHO STILL NEEDS THEIR MONEY BUT NOT THEIR ADVICE

TOW BOOKS
www.towbooks.com
Cincinnati, Ohio

SARAH WALKER

11   10   09   08   07   5 4 3 2 1

Distributed in Canada by Fraser Direct, 100 Armstrong Avenue Georgetown, ON, Canada L7G 5S4, Tel: (905) 877-4411; Distributed in the U.K. and Europe by David & Charles, Brunel House, Newton Abbot, Devon, TQ12 4PU, England, Tel: (+44) 1626 323200, Fax: (+44) 1626 323319, E-mail: postmaster@davidandcharles.co.uk; Distributed in Australia by Capricorn Link, P.O. Box 704, Windsor, NSW 2756 Australia, Tel: (02) 4577-3555

Library of Congress Cataloging-in-Publication Data

Walker, Sarah W.
  Really, you've done enough : a parents' guide to stop parenting their adult child who still needs their money but not their advice / by Sarah Walker. -- 1st ed.
     p. cm.
  ISBN 978-1-58297-478-1 (pbk. : alk. paper)
  1. Adult children living with parents--Humor. 2. Parent and adult child--Humor. 3. Family--Humor. 4. Intergenerational relations-- Humor. I. Title.
  HQ755.86.W35 2007
  306.874--dc22
                                                          2007018623

Edited by John Warner and Jane Friedman
Designed by Claudean Wheeler
Illustrations by Ben Patrick
Hijiki image by Steven Mark Needham/Jupiterimages
Production coordinated by Mark Griffin

fw
F+W PUBLICATIONS, INC.

DEDICATION

For all those who are f—ed up and
for those who love them. In other
words, this book is for everyone.

CONTENTS

INTRODUCTION
You Fuck Them Up[1]

I think some congratulations are in order. You, as a parent, have managed to produce and raise a child who has made it to their mid twenties, maybe even late twenties[2]—and although they could stand to lose anywhere from three to ten pounds—falls within a normal Body Mass Index. They also love you so much that they understand why you would want to give them money. They know what joy it would bring you to have them crash in your basement for a couple of months, rent-free, in order to ease your empty-nest syndrome. The fact that you didn't suffer from empty-nest syndrome when they left for college is a testament to their sensitivity in coming home as often as possible for meals and laundry services so you would not feel abandoned.

---

[1] Read Philip Larkin's poem "This Be the Verse." I would have reprinted it here but I couldn't get the rights. Seriously, it's super hard to get reprint rights. And expensive! I would have had to pay for them for not only the United States but also Britain where everything costs, like, double. However, it was cool to e-mail a publishing house in London, there was something so classily international about it. Anyway, if you read the poem, you'll see that I'm not just being vulgar. Inspired by Larkin's poem, I originally wanted to name this book *You Can Stop Fucking Me Up Now*. I thought the kids would like that. However, when this understandably proved to be a no-go, even after I pointed out that if I substituted asterisks or "effing" for "fucking," it might prove to be less offensive. Therefore, I have made use of the word "fuck" as much as possible in this book. You're welcome.

[2] Very impressive.

You have also raised a very intelligent child, as they are intimately familiar with cutting-edge scientific discoveries. For example, it has recently been noted by major publications and Danish scientists wearing monocles that, financially, twenty-eight is the new twenty-one! Your child is very excited about this, as it sort of implies time travel, or at least the stoppage of time. It is as though your child is entering a deep freeze for seven years where they do not need to tend to themselves and at the end of this period, will emerge un-aged and well rested and with a high-paying job, maybe even some minor fame/notoriety. You, as a good parent, must do everything in your power to assure your child that this may actually be true. Please do not consider this to be delusional and unhealthy, it is merely good parenting by way of supporting your child's dreams. Dreams, by definition, are just that: fantasies that will probably never come true, but without striving towards these unattainable dreams, your child will never reach their greatest potential. Therefore, if you disabuse them of the Financial-Age Time-Stoppage Dream, you might as well be telling them to give up on this game we call Life.

Here is a chart to better explain this Financial Age Time Stoppage:

ACTUAL AGE	FINANCIAL AGE
7	7
14	14
21	14
28	21

I should note that Emotional Age is a different matter entirely. This will be a useful reference tool with your son and daughter.

MALE ACTUAL AGE	MALE EMOTIONAL AGE
7	7
14	7
21	7
28	7
FEMALE ACTUAL AGE	**FEMALE EMOTIONAL AGE**
7	7
14	14
21	21
28	42

If you have a financially independent child, the above Financial-Age Time-Stoppage Chart means nothing to you. You have probably also never seen a rain cloud and have perfect pitch, you are so lucky. You should treat a financially independent child with the utmost respect, as the money you save on them will allow you to buy venti chai lattes with reckless abandon and give money to street performers. Whereas before you would take out a stopwatch to see if the human statue covered in silver paint blinked within two minutes before you would give him a dime, now you can, without breaking stride, flick a quarter into his hat and maybe give him a little wink, to which he will instinctively wink back. In the past, a wink from an alleged statue would have been a deal breaker and you would have taken your quarter back after yelling, "Ah-ha!" Now, though, because of your financially independent child, you are rolling in it, and can continue, whistling, on your merry way, definitely not caring that the human-statue street person failed to possess sufficient discipline to resist returning a wink, thus perhaps explaining why he is a common street performer, instead of a Cirque du Soleil troupe member, or at least associated with a lesser circus. I mean, it would be really hard to be a part of Cirque du Soleil.

However, these are the lives of very *very* few parents, and if you are not such a parent, you should not be distressed. Who needs to give money to human statues anyway? Your child is the neediest of all human statues, as it were, and if your child is an actual street-performing human statue, that goes doubly for you. Parental support should come in the form of monetary funds, for I believe your actual parenting in the form of advice, guidance, and notes to your child's Tech Ed teacher about her strong hylephobia (fear of wood), which would keep her from participating in class so she wouldn't have to see the boy who dumped her every day, has reached it's full potential. Now, this may be hard, but perhaps in the peripheral regions of your brain you have noticed that your child, though grown up, does not necessarily have it all together. The technical term for this is, brace yourself, "fucked up." I'm sorry to say it, but your child is probably more fucked up than you realize, and one of the contributing factors may be that you provided them with enough health insurance and laundry services growing up so that now they wander the streets of New York, drunk and uninsured, as they have been unable to find an adequate health-insurance provider on their own, and must spend more money than they ought to on friendly neighborhood laundry places. This is all the more reason to provide them with enough money so that they may continue to patronize this friendly neighborhood laundry place, which, no matter what their mood, always brings a smile to their face and makes them feel like they've accomplished something when, the next day, they pick up a bag of freshly folded clothes and towels.

Perhaps you did indeed do a good job of raising your child, but you should not expect them to tell you that. I would never tell my parents that they did a good job raising me, although they clearly did. Look at me now, writing a book! Right now you might be saying, yes, but she's writing a book about how parents never stop fucking you up, therefore, I must assume that her parents fucked her up. Well, assume away, Assumey-Face! But I'm writing the book, not you, so my parents must have done something right, even if it was unintentional. Great, this book is going to do horribly now. I can't believe I just jinxed myself like that. Excuse me.

I have composed myself. Forget all of that, this is not about me, it's about you. As your child will never tell you one way or the other if you did a good job in raising them, you are in a constant state of limbo, but if you follow the advice in this book, you will never need assurance from your child, as the following pages will hone your parenting skills in such a manner that your child will begin to believe that you are the good parent that you actually are. If I do my job right, your child will so appreciate your new skills that they will visit you 50 percent more of the time in the nursing home, which will be nicer than they initially expected to spring for. (Again, do not expect them to actually come out and say that you are a good parent.) No, they will not ask you to live with them, as with your newly honed parenting skills you will understand what a terrible imposition that would be for them and probably ruin their marriage. By the way, don't worry, they'll totally get married. I mean, they won't end up dying alone just because they haven't had a serious relationship yet and they're already twenty-five years old. I mean, seriously, did they want me to marry the sixty-year-old professor who told me that he had a fear of aging as he stroked my hand and then put his head on my neck during a lingering hug? Twenty-five is the new eighteen, and that would be screwed up if I, I mean, your child were married at eighteen, so stop freaking out, okay??? Excuse me.

I'm back. Before you delve into this book you must approach it with an open mind and be ready to admit most of your faults as I lay them out for you. For example, if I were to point out to my parents that perhaps they should not have conveyed the news of the demise of Major, our beloved family dog, over email, I would expect them to nod sagely and say, "Yes, Sarah, that may not have been the most sensitive way to tell you of Major's passing. Next time we shall call you. Now here is one hundred, no, two hundred dollars … and a diamond bracelet." Therefore, if your family dog does pass away[3], please follow the example of this hypothetical situation in which I'm sure my parents wish they would have reacted thusly. If you need any more advice regarding this specific hypothetical situation, you could always email me, or better yet, send me one to two hundred dollars … and a diamond bracelet, if you have one. If you don't have one, I understand from television commercials that there are many stores that sell diamonds, and the people who buy them are very attractive and live in large apartments and go on trips to Rome and listen to classical music. Therefore, please buy me a diamond bracelet so that I may assume this fabulous lifestyle. I assure you that you will be the better parent for it.

---

[3] They need not be named "Major," though I do recommend it as a dog name. Actually, don't steal my dead dog's name, that's creepy.

THEN AND NOW
Your Twenties vs.
Your Child's Twenties

Right now you may be thinking, "Listen, I know what it's like to be in one's twenties. I lived through my own twenties." Good point. However, things have vastly changed since you grew up in the halcyon days of quilting bees and barn-raising dances. Here is a brief overview of the differences between then and now.

FASHION

THEN: You wore bathing suits that covered every inch of skin, including the face, save for two holes cut out around the nostrils and one at the mouth. Straws were inserted into the mouth hole for easier breathing. These suits were worn at all times, not just at the beach or poolside.

NOW: We wear synthetic fibers woven from moonstone and Teflon, which feel and breathe like cotton. These garments, are, of course, bullet-proof. As a result, gun laws have grown lax so that we may go around shooting people in the groin at will for amusement.

HOUSING

THEN: Every house had 2.5 rooms, the .5th room reserved for their freakish half-child, who, though it completed the nuclear-family ideal, remained a source of shame.

NOW: Everyone lives in individual sun domes that contain only orchids and waterfalls, while outside, civil war rages. We travel from sun dome to sun dome on giant zip cords.

TRANSPORTATION

THEN: You rode on the backs of giant carrier pigeons, but the continual strain on their backs led to their eventual extinction.

NOW: We travel on the backs of bald eagles, which is the main cause of their status on the endangered species list.

LITERATURE

THEN: Novels appeared in tiny tiny print in serial form on the backs of baseball cards. A stick of gum was included in each package of baseball cards to enhance the reading experience, but it was found that it just contributed to the headache brought on by straining to read such small type.

NOW: Each new novel is first written in skywriting form and hastily recorded by a group of stenographers before the clouds dissipate.

VERNACULAR

THEN: You spoke in a mixture of French sign language and Esperanto.

NOW: Everyone speaks with an affected Katharine Hepburn accent, except when a Spanish word, like "tacos," comes up. Then we pronounce it with an extremely affected Spanish accent.

WEATHER

THEN: Every day was seventy-two degrees and sunny, except for Christmas, when exactly eight inches of powdery snow fell, beginning at noon on Christmas Eve, and ending at midnight on Christmas night.

NOW: The ozone is covered in a protective shield, which scientists believed would halt global warming, but instead it became a disastrous, irreversible blocker of the sun. Your child has not seen nor felt sunlight in fifteen years and Highlanders roam the Earth.

FOOD

THEN: Lunch consisted of turtle soup in a thermos and a single boiled quail's egg.

NOW: Everyone thinks about food for half an hour, decides it's not worth it to ingest dangerously fattening calories, and chugs an energy drink.

MUSIC

THEN: People fell asleep to the song of a nightingale in a gilded cage, accompanied by a music box.

NOW: We listen to the sound of a chair being scraped over a rug and enjoy it, "ironically," as long as attractive British people are doing the scraping.

ART

THEN: People arranged themselves in elaborate re-creations of neo-classical paintings, focusing primarily on the works of David, and it was considered one's civic duty to pose thusly for a total of eighty hours a year.

NOW: Everything is considered art and is protected by stringent copyright laws, which is the excuse your neighbor frequently uses when he doesn't pick up his dog's poop.

HUMOR

THEN: Your jokes were entirely Charles Schultz-based, and came either from *Peanuts* or personal Chuck Schultz interactions and anecdotes. (Example: Remember when Chuck got so drunk he tried to make out with the waitress?? Man, Chuck was a wild man!)

NOW: We are told to enjoy old footage of dogs and cats wearing human clothes and walking on their hind legs, as well as modern footage of squirrels on jet skis, but we wonder why our souls feel like they are dying.

PETS

THEN: Wolves were kept for protection and were taught how to make breakfast and keep house. They wore aprons and embroidered hand towels that read "Bless This Mess."

NOW: The Wolves have become unruly and steal our breakfasts and sweep the dust under the rug and snigger when they see embroidered hand towels.

INTERIOR DECORATING

THEN: Everyone had a parlor with red velvet wallpaper and an antler chandelier. You spent the majority of the morning receiving guests while sitting on a settee, and the majority of the afternoon in a breakfast nook, catching up on your correspondence.

NOW: Each room is vacuum-sealed and lit in the neon light that matches your mood. Chinchilla-fur couches are all the rage and people are paid to stand in plantlike poses.

ACCEPTABLE MODES OF COMMUNICATION

THEN: A series of tin cans connected by string were used for local calls and high-powered telepathy machines were used for cross-continental and international calls. The series of strings that criss-crossed the sky also contributed to the fate of the carrier pigeon, as they would be frequently clothes-lined and fall to the ground, lifeless.

NOW: Morse code communicated through girlish slapping.

EXERCISE

THEN: Done mostly with a skipping rope, a medicine ball, and the imbibing of juniper-berry shakes. Other forms of exercise included vigorous manly handshakes and the shouting of brusque encouragements to "Go! Fight! Win!"

NOW: Now we only exercise our minds with mathematical exercises focusing on string theory and chaos theory. And we're fat-asses.

ROOM TEMPERATURE

THEN: 68.2 degrees Fahrenheit.

NOW: 71.5 degrees Fahrenheit.

SOFT DRINKS

THEN: Sarsaparilla.

NOW: Liquid heroin.

TYPES OF COMFORTERS

THEN: Stuffed with goose down and Pegasus feathers.

NOW: Stuffed with nails and rose petals.

FONTS

THEN: Elaborate Gothic-style calligraphy.

NOW: Everything is written in invisible ink and only by following a series of clues written on secret maps can you read any text.

SPACE TRAVEL

THEN: Frowned upon.

NOW: Totally acceptable.

COMPUTERS

THEN: Soothsayers.

NOW: Purveyors of Truth.

CUPCAKE SIZE

THEN: Adorably bite-sized.

NOW: Intimidating.

LIVING AT HOME
The Good Old Days ... Today!

I lived at home for six months when I was between jobs and needed to save money. My parents made me do the grocery shopping and the laundry, even though I had no experience in either field. Therefore, I cannot be blamed for the subsequent trichinosis and bedbug outbreak in my home, which I believe were the results not of my ineptitude, but of a lack of foresight on my parents' part.

— "Swwalker"

So your child has chosen to live with you post-college while they find their footing. The process of finding one's footing can take anywhere from three months to eight years, so for God's sake, don't rush them. The worst thing you could do is destabilize them just when they feel as though they have found solid ground from which to launch out into the world. You learned this lesson when you watched *Indiana Jones and the Last Crusade* with your child that summer of '94, when McDonald's was offering a special promotion over a three-week period of a free VHS copy of part of the Indiana Jones trilogy (part one the first week and so on) every time you purchased an Extra Value Meal. By the way, do you think it was really worth it to get those tapes for free, now that you know how bad McDonald's is for growing children, compounded by the fact that VCRs are now obsolete? Maybe you should think about that. Anyway, as you know from watching the trilogy, in *Indiana Jones and the Last Crusade*, as part of a test to get to the Holy Grail, Indiana has to literally take a leap of faith and step out into a chasm with nothing below him, but because he has faith an invisible bridge appears. The metaphor should be obvious to you by now: You should be that invisible bridge that kept Indy (your child) from falling to a certain death. Invisible and supportive, unlike Sean Connery, who plays Indy's father in the movie and is nothing but trouble! In fact, Steven Spielberg's *Indiana Jones and the Last Crusade* could be seen as an allegory for the post-college pre-marriage parent-child relationship as told through a madcap adventure story involving immortal crusaders and Nazis.

What does one do as an invisible bridge of support? You must provide your child with three hearty yet nutritious meals a day, laundry services, and the use of an automobile, preferably an environmentally responsible one, as your child will have to live in this world after you leave it so if you could not pollute it any more that would be super. A separate entrance or perhaps even a carriage house/pool house/apartment above a garage à la Kirk Cameron's character, Mike Seaver, in *Growing Pains* would be ideal. If you never watched *Growing Pains* with your child, just know that Mike's parents, though strict when they had to put up with his high jinks, at the end of each episode provided him with love and wisdom, but even if they hadn't, the sweet apartment above the garage said more than words ever could. Well, Alan Thicke did have a way with words, but very few people can pull off a Thicke. Did you know that Alan Thicke wrote the theme song to *Growing Pains*? Well, he did. Thicke is so cool. He also wrote the theme to *The Facts of Life*. And Michael Jackson's *Thriller* album. And "Amazing Grace."

If you begin to feel nervous at the notion that your child does not "have their own place" or "live their own independent life," just relax. Think of it as college ... for you! Don't you miss the good old days when you could hang out with your friends in the common room and over a bottle or three of cheap Chianti or maybe some illicit substances discuss life and love and war or whatever you hippies talked about in the seventies? Or maybe if you worked your entire life in order to give your child the college experience you never had, consider this an opportunity to make good on a missed opportunity. Think of your child as the loveable prankster/slacker in every college movie. The one who provides comic relief and at whom you just can't stay mad at because man is he charming! This could work for a girl, but not as well, as historically, girls do not play the loveable prankster/slacker in movies, which, though regrettable, is just the way it is. If your child is a stay-at-home girl, think of her as an Emily Dickinson type: very talented, reclusive, sensitive, maybe gay. Just kidding, your daughter probably isn't gay. But if she is, she is so like Emily Dickinson! Take a look through her things when she isn't around and you'll probably find some rhyming poetry in her journal. If it doesn't rhyme then that's okay too, it's just not very Dickinson and is probably not poetry. I don't care what they say, if it doesn't rhyme, it's not poetry.

If you're a father, ideally your stay-at-home child is your son. He probably has all sorts of plans to play tricks on the square old dean (your wife) who has been making all the stupid rules. You can go on bra and panty raids to the girls' college next door by propping a ladder up to the window and sneaking in while they all have pillow fights in the next room, and organize mixers with them where you drink gin-and-tonics and play the ukulele. No girls' college next door? That's weird. Well, watch porn instead! Ew, don't do that. Seriously, it is completely inappropriate and creepy to watch porn with your son. You should have already known this, that's really bad that you had to be told that. On the other hand, a good old-fashioned mother-daughter porn fest might be just be what the doctor ordered. Tearing down the social stigmas surrounding pornography will result in a frank and open conversation about sex and the terrible festishization of women that is rampant in our culture, topics that have been glossed over or hardly discussed at all in conversations between you and your daughter thus far. After all, you're both intelligent adults! Also, this is a great way to find out if your stay-at-home daughter is gay or not. If she digs the lesbian porn, well, you can draw your own conclusions.[1]

---

[1] If you conclude that your stay-at-home daughter is indeed a lesbian, you may pat yourself on the back for having such a sexually progressive child, one who is the subject of many male fantasies and yet, at the same time, is immune to their masculine charms. She's like a superhero, really.

Perhaps the discrepancy between how you should treat a stay-at-home son as opposed to a stay-at-home daughter sounds a tad sexist to you. Good, that was a test! You should treat your son and/or daughter equally. (Again, acknowledging that your daughter could probably not play the role of the charming prankster/slacker, though you never know.) If you have the crazy notion that your child should have to pay rent in their childhood home (you bastard), maybe you should remember how upset you were when they left for college. Your empty-nest syndrome was so acute you drove three hours to see their Ultimate Frisbee team play on Saturdays and, because you were so happy to see them, you never questioned the nerdy nature of the "sport" and even ignored the specter of your failed dreams of them becoming a professional athlete and ultimately buying you a house. So why are you complaining now? Cherish these moments with your child. Who knows when they'll find their own place or decide to take a backpacking trip to Iceland and leave home forever when they fall in love with someone who looks like Bjork? Then you'll have to go to Iceland to visit them, and you know how you don't like volcanic islands.

LIVING AT HOME: DIFFERENT TYPES OF STAY-AT-HOME CHILDREN

There are actually two types of stay-at-home children. The first is the smart, thoughtful child who has not as of yet decided exactly what they want to do with their life. In the meantime they are saving money by living at home. They have an active social life and are working towards an ultimate goal of moving to a major metropolis to share an overpriced apartment with friends. They are probably the type of child who will more than likely participate in college-like high jinks with you.

The second type of stay-at-home child is a loser, possibly a drug addict/dealer, who can't pull their shit together and will mooch off of you for as long as humanly possible. A child of this type can't be the smartest person ever. I mean, maybe they aren't a drug dealer. They could just be insanely socially awkward and afraid of human interaction outside of the safe boundaries of their childhood home, and be sort of sporadically smart, in that they know a lot about computers or video games. Or, they could be a savant like Dustin Hoffman in *Rain Man*, and, when asked, can immediately say that March 20, 1880, fell on a Saturday (if it gets around that they can do that they'll probably be asked a lot), but they are certainly not street-smart by any means, because if they were, they definitely would not be living with you. Well, that is, unless you're some sort of super-billionaire who owns a sports team and who provides them with their own wing of your giant Dallas mansion, complete with tennis court and swimming pool with an adjacent barbecue ensconced in a gazebo. Then your child would be the opposite of smart (stupid) if they did not live with you and invite all of their friends over for delicious poolside barbecue.

There is a subtle difference between a non-stay-at-home unemployed child and an unemployed child who is living at home. For a child not living at home, unemployment merely provides the necessary buildup to the exciting drama of when your child eventually gets that job and rises through the ranks from the mailroom to the boardroom in the span of three weeks and has a tumultuous affair with the boss's wife. However, a child who lives at home can potentially have a job, but is invariably stymied by self-doubt and still attached to the metaphorical parental teat. If said teat is not metaphorical, man did you fuck up your kid! There is nothing I can do for you at this point, seriously, put down the book, I don't want anything to do with you. That's gross. It sounds like a horror film, and not like a Sarah Michelle Gellar horror film either, more like a really weird *People Under the Stairs*-ish horror film. However, if we're all talking about a metaphorical teat, then you should employ some metaphorical vinegar and apply it to your metaphorical teat so that your non-metaphorical child may be metaphorically repulsed and hence be metaphorically weaned off the metaphorical teat. This was a bad metaphor. My apologies. I'm new at this advice game. What is this, like, page ten? I'll get better, probably.

A Message from the Author

Perhaps you are thinking to yourself right now, "Why is there a separate message from the author when the entire book is the author directly talking to me?" Well, it's because I want to take off my advice-giving turtleneck and sit Indian style and talk to you, person to person, in a relaxed fashion. I'm glad we're comfortable. Feel free to ask me anything. Oh, I see. Your question is "Why should I be taking advice from some upstart kid who doesn't know the first thing about being a parent?" Well, let me tell you something. I am an upstart and sort of a kid and very much not a parent. So. Your point is well taken. Here are some things you should know about me in order to assuage your fears that you are being led down a primrose path by a blind person with cotton in her ears.

1. I dabble in sorcery. This means that I know things that others do not know, and I am older than my age belies. In fact, sorcery is older than time. Therefore, by the transitive property, I too am very old and wise.

2. My parents were divorced when I was twenty-three, and two plus three is five, which is a prime number, of which there are an infinite number, similar to the infinite amount of advice that I can bestow upon you.

3. I recently saw on *Animal Planet* what a dolphin with an erection looks like, and it frightened me. Previously I had not been afraid of dolphins. This means that I am a very sensitive person who, given compelling evidence, is willing to change her opinion.

4. *Clue* is my favorite movie. This means that I appreciate both humor and solving mysteries. I believe it is clear how this would relate to giving parental advice.

5. Admitting that *Clue* is my favorite movie and not lying and saying that something else, like, say, Jean Renoir's *The Rules of the Game* is my favorite movie means that I have no qualms about being completely honest with you, even if it means sacrificing my dignity, as long as I can couple said sacrifice with a pretentious reference.

6. That being said, my favorite sex scene in a movie (because you're probably wondering) is the kitchen sex scene in Bertolucci's *The Dreamers.* This scene is not for the faint of heart, in that it involves a kitchen floor and a sibling looking on whilst making eggs. Don't worry, they're French. The fact that I just shared that with you means that I can talk about adult matters in an adult fashion and am paying forward a very sexy scene.

You should appreciate this, because mentioning sex to parents is very difficult for me. However, I just did so, which clearly shows that I embrace difficulty with aplomb.

7. I get second-hand embarrassment very, very easily. This means that if I see someone doing something embarrassing, like participating in the reality TV show *Celebrity Fit Club*, I feel acute embarrassment myself. This means that I am very empathetic and can relate to you and your parental problems.

8. I love raw organic cashews. That has nothing to do with the advice, but if you like my book, you may send me a gift basket of raw organic cashews, as they are very expensive and would make a nice thank-you gift.

Now that you know a little more about me, I hope we can continue on together in this marvelous journey, preferably with a sandwich bag full of raw organic cashews.

ACCEPTABLE CHILDHOOD MYTHS TO STILL INSIST ARE TRUE TO YOUR ADULT CHILD

Every parent lets their child believe in certain myths that add to the mystery and excitement of childhood. Santa Claus, for example. Over time, obviously, these myths are dispelled and your child is left with the harsh, cold reality that no strange, bearded, morbidly obese man will visit them in the middle of the night once a year. However, there are certain myths of which you should never disabuse your child. These myths help them deal with difficult situations and provide a comforting familiarity in the face of the unknown. Here are some of the childhood myths that you should try in every possible way to keep real in the mind of your adult child.

GRANDPA'S GHOST LIVES IN A BOTTLE OF WILD TURKEY

When your child was eight years old their grandfather died. At the funeral, you whispered to your spouse that rather than his eternal soul residing in heaven, more likely your father-in-law's soul was residing in a bottle of Wild Turkey. Your eight-year-old heard this, and took it as truth. However true or untrue it may be—I mean, who knows if there really is a heaven and if heaven for

Grandpa would be inside a bottle of Wild Turkey, à la *I Dream of Jeannie?*—it has been something of a social crutch for your child at parties. When asked to do shots of Wild Turkey, they are able to use the following excuse without irony: "My grandpa's ghost is in there." Yes, this has severely hampered many of their relationships, but it has drastically curbed their drinking, as they suspect that other people's grandparents' ghosts live in other liquor bottles, and they are a healthier person for it. Well, healthy in body, I mean. They're obviously considered sort of crazy, but that's their "thing," and they're completely normal in every other aspect of life. Except that they're totally lame at parties.

SNOW SHARKS

We are all familiar with the myth of the Snow Shark. Every snowfall, the Snow Sharks emerge from their underground cocoons, where they have been drinking brandy, and terrorize suburban lawns, nipping the ankles of small children. The only sign of their presence is a tiny gray dorsal fin, cutting swaths through the freshly fallen snow.

Snow Sharks are terrifying indeed, and jerks when they're drunk, which they usually are. Sometimes they even make their way into backyard swimming pools when the water is cool, usually before Memorial Day and after Labor Day. The myth of the Snow Shark has terrorized your child to this day, but it always kept them out of trouble on snow days as a child. When their other friends were out throwing snowballs at cars, your child was cowering in their room, watching out their window for signs of the dreaded Snow Sharks, praying for their friends' safety. Now that they're an adult, this fear of Snow Sharks has kept them away from skiing and snowboarding, two of the most dangerous and expensive sports. They also live in a warm climate where they will never have any fear of Snow Sharks, providing an excellent getaway for you in the winter months.

THE NATIVE AMERICAN IN THE LINEN CLOSET

Based on the popular children's novel *The Indian in the Cupboard*, this childhood myth said that whenever your child opened the linen closet to get sheets to make their

own bed, a tiny Native American astride a tiny buffalo would jump atop the sheets and help them make their bed. No, this never actually happened to your child, but there was always hope. You told them that the tiny Native American astride the tiny buffalo never visited them because they could not fold their sheets with proper hospital corners, and until they could achieve that, they were not worthy to change linens with our noble, tiny, magical ancestors and their noble, tiny, magical beasts. Henceforth, your child has always striven to perfect the hospital corners on their bed, religiously washes and changes their sheets once a week, and is known for their meticulous and sweet-smelling beds.

WITCH BALLS

Witch balls are beautifully blown glass balls, traditionally hung in windows to ward off evil witches, who, attracted by the colorful and graceful design of the balls, become curious and investigate them and then are trapped inside by the special power of the balls. This, of course, is retarded. However, you  taught your child that witches lived in the witch balls that hung in every window of your house, and if they ever mishandled the balls, the witches would be released and perform an irreversible hex on them. This led your child to always handle every type of ball with special delicacy, which led to impressive basketball skills. Because of their increased ball sensitivity and awareness, they have been able to sustain many a relationship with their amazing ball-juggling abilities.

LADY IN THE WATER

The myth of the Lady in the Water states that when one stays too long in the bathtub or shower, a fearsome lady will emerge, wrinkled and pale, and demand a sponge bath from whoever is taking too long in the bath or shower. The fervent belief in this myth has kept your child

from wasting water, and they have never caused a roommate or live-in significant other to once be mad at them for taking too long in the bathroom. They are also deathly afraid of taking baths

and showers, so sometimes they go weeks without bathing, but a good dosage of fear is healthy now and again.

The myth of the Lady in the Water has been disseminated over the years, most notably by M. Night Shyamalan's feature film of the same name. The origins of the myth have largely been lost to Hollywood reimaginings and incorrect use of the popular phrase "Find your own Lady in the Water," which has become as ubiquitous as "Didn't *The Village* suck?" Nowadays, the myth has been so corroded that many believe it's simply a cute colloquialism that means "Go wash Grandma." However, it has increasingly been used to express annoyance at another person, annoyance so intense that you think the guilty party should leave the room and perform an unpleasant task (presumably, washing Grandma), as in "Stop talking and go find your own Lady in the Water."

UNEMPLOYMENT
Motorcycle Gangs and Nobel Prizes

When I was out of work, my parents helped me out with a monthly stipend. This was very generous of them—in fact, too generous, as I was able to take this stipend and form a small vigilante gang of rogues that scoured the Southwest in a giant yellow school bus, knocking down mailboxes and handing out knuckle sandwiches. Literally—they were made of pigs' knuckles and they were disgusting. People would gag, and sometimes even vomit. The time I spent on the bus severely cut back on the time I had to spend solving the global-warming crisis and that's why we are all on a one-way ticket to a living hell on Earth.

— "Walker, Sarah"

So your son or daughter is unemployed. Well done!

While other people's children are off attending law school, trading stocks, or teaching first-graders how to read, your child has refused to sell their soul to some corporate overlord and devote their life to filthy, filthy lucre. In this respect, you have done well. You have taught your child to look beyond monetary wealth and appreciate what is most important in life: Free Time.

However, before you pat yourself on the back for having an unemployed child, there's something you should know. In this Free Time, your child has the opportunity to reflect on their upbringing and perhaps dwell on some of the reasons that led them to this unemployed state, however glorious the basking in Free Time might be. For example, however well-intentioned your motives were, forcing them to take a summer job painting their grandfather's house may have put them off employment forever, what with the rabid raccoons and Grandpa's constant bayonet lessons. Anyway, here is a highly scientific graph to better demonstrate this concept of the direct relationship between free time and reflection on your parental mistakes. Notice how similar it is to the concept of

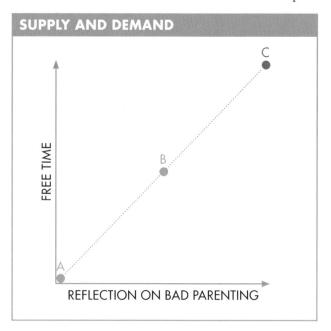

SUPPLY AND DEMAND

FREE TIME

REFLECTION ON BAD PARENTING

supply and demand, a staple of the business world, which is a place where people with jobs work. Ironic, no?

As one can clearly see, the ideal amount of Free Time lies on point B of the graph. How does one reach point B? The answer: Provide your child with a stipend that will allow them to maintain the perfect balance of thinking and free time. And by "stipend," I mean "money."

You obviously want your child to contemplate important issues such as the environment and pandas and whatnot. Maybe when they don't have what fascists call a "job," they could solve global warming! That's a hot (get it?) issue nowadays. Your child would be famous if they solved the global-warming crisis! Wouldn't that be great? You'd be the parent of a world-renowned scientist, which would be doubly as impressive, since your child likely received no scientific training while they were getting that degree in American Genre Art, 1790–1820. They would probably win the Nobel Prize, and then you would be able to enjoy all the benefits of riding the coattails of fame, starting with the black-tie Nobel ceremony in Stockholm, where you will probably meet the king of Sweden. This would be followed by fancy vacations to private island resorts and immediate entrance to the most exclusive restaurants in town, where you would meet all the A-list Hollywood celebrities, who care about the environment and who each own seven electric cars and a free-range chicken ranch within the confines of their Malibu compounds, and who have glaciers imported from Peru, which they preserve with state-of-the-art air conditioning in their living rooms. When you are hobnobbing with movie stars, who are congratulating you on raising such an amazingly brilliant child, now World's Leading Scientist and Nobel Prize Winner, maybe you'll end up in the pages of a weekly tabloid as an unknown friend of a celebrity, which, while preserving your anonymity and protecting you from the incessant hounding by the paparazzi and an eventual nervous breakdown, will look very nice in that little scrapbook that you keep. All of this you could have if you provide your child with just enough money to sit in a comfortable chair and contemplate and ultimately solve the problem of global warming.

However, if you provide your unemployed child with too much money, they'll go out and buy a motorcycle and a leather vest and join a motorcycle gang and wreak havoc across the Midwest. All of this will culminate when an unsuspecting teenage tourist seeking directions at a roadside diner leans up against the first bike in a row of your child's motorcycle gang's bikes, or "rides," and, in a domino effect, the entire row comes tumbling down and your child is one of the twenty in the gang who assault the tourist and, although lax, the small-town cops who have been coincidentally eating lunch at that very same diner manage to arrest only *your* child after the rest of the gang scatters, abandoning your child, who up until that moment considered the gang to be his best friends. The police will triumphantly throw your child in the county jail, which has only two cells, one for local drunks and one for local whores. Who knows which one your child will land in? It depends on how the police are feeling that day.

What's important to this story is that, either way, you'll never get a grandchild out of that mess. Your only hope is that this happens to your son and, while in jail, he finds Jesus and falls in love with one of the local whores, who has, coincidentally, also found Jesus, and they start a new life and family together. If you have a daughter, same thing, only one of the local (male) drunks will have to have coincidentally also found Jesus. Then you'll have a Jesus-freak child who lives with an ex-criminal, but, by God, you'll get that grandkid.

On the other hand, if you provide your child with just the right amount of money to solve global warming, they'll probably marry a liberal movie star and you'll get at least three grandchildren before the marriage goes horribly awry, unless your child can solve something else, like how to stop earthquakes. If they do indeed figure out how to stop earthquakes, the ensuing media frenzy will most likely keep their movie-star spouse close, since, let's be honest, they aren't getting any younger, despite the plastic surgery, and Hollywood is a youth market and they could use all the publicity they can get.

The correct amount of money provided for your unemployed child should cover such indulgences as jazz records and cashmere socks. These items will provide a comfortable atmosphere conducive to solving the world's problems and not thinking about theirs as they relate to you. Here is a visual aid to better demonstrate this.

TOO LITTLE MONEY:
child sprawled on couch

TOO MUCH MONEY:
motorcycle gang

JUST THE RIGHT AMOUNT:
celebrity couple

UNEMPLOYMENT
Creative Child vs.
Uncreative Child

Writing is a job. Really. Even though I'm just staying at home and sometimes go on long walks, I'm always writing. In my head, or on a small notepad that I periodically bring out in front of large groups of people so that they may know that I just had a brilliant idea that I must jot down before it disappears into the ether and someone else thinks of it. You know what? I think you're just jealous.

— "Sarah"

In the event that your child is a creative person who posits that they are working (writing, painting, weaving) even though they are technically unemployed, more monies are needed to sustain them.

Creative people think *constantly*. It's a burden, really, the amount of thinking they do, mostly about themselves and existentialism and shit like that. If you are the parent of a creative person, you are in big trouble, because, inevitably, all roads of deep introspection lead back to you.

Here is a sample chain of thought of an unemployed twentysomething creative person:

> I'm hungry. → I should cook to save money. → I don't know how to cook. → My parents cooked too much for me, leading to my extreme hunger at this moment. → I shall make a creative sandwich.

Here is a sample chain of thought of an unemployed twenty-something uncreative person:

> I'm hungry. → I have no food. → I have no idea what to do in this situation. → My parents produced food, as if by magic. → I shall remain hungry, as I do not know any magic.

Notice the subtle difference between a creative person and an uncreative person: the creative person creates a plan to stave off hunger, whereas the uncreative person is borderline retarded and would have never survived in pioneer times. On the plus side, they would never have been accused of being a witch in colonial times. However, both suffer the same ultimate fate. This is an important lesson in the value of creativity as well, in that creativity and idiocy are ultimately one and the same. You may impart that knowledge to your child and pass it off as your own if you like.[1]

The advantages of having a creative child are clear. They are more likely to think of the solution to global warming faster than an uncreative child. Although there is a 90 percent (scientifically proven) chance

---

[1] That was a test. Creativity and idiocy are actually opposite things. If you actually did pass that knowledge off as your own, what a terrible parent you must be. Also, you should really stop imparting wisdom at this point, especially if it's clearly false and stolen.

that, either way, given the right amount of money, as discussed before, your unemployed child will indeed save the world from environmental disaster, a creative child will do this more quickly and with more moxie than an uncreative child.

For example, a creative child will probably adopt a superhero persona, like Captain Planet, only less gay, and stop the evil industrialists from polluting our air and oceans. They will create their own catch phrase, like "Save the environment? Plan (on) it!" And when they catch the evil industrialist who was trying to escape, they'll dangle the perspiring villain above a huge barrel of toxic waste that they keep in their evil factory and say, "Looks like you need to cool off."

They will also fashion a well-tailored (but not gay-seeming) outfit that they can change into in the blink of an eye.

They won't necessarily seek out the media, but their exploits will be known far and wide both for the flair with which they are carried out and for the underlying wit and generosity of all of their actions, which will culminate in the end of global warming and be made into a feature film, starring their celebrity spouse.

However, if your child is uncreative, they'll probably sit on their comfortable chair in their cashmere socks, listening to an Art Tatum record, and fiddle around with equations and think of some scientific way to solve global warming. They will publish their lengthy thesis in Scientific American, where it will be read by other scientists, who will in turn apply your child's methods to the betterment of the environment. Yaaaaaaawn. Where's the panache, the showmanship, in that solution? Sometimes it's really the journey that matters most in life[2], and your uncreative child will have missed out on that fantastic ride.

---

[2] This is a cliché, and, like most clichés, it, though true, should be repeat-ed sparingly and only when necessary, such as now, when discussing a superhero route to solving global warming.

YOUR CHILD'S FIRST JOB
Take a Picture on Their First Day and Make an Ornament Out of It

My first job was as a tour guide at a major network television station. I guided five tours of thirty people a day, six days a week. As a consequence, my tour-guide uniform began to stink, as I never had the opportunity to dry-clean it. Where were my parents when I needed them most? Oh, they were at "home," working at their own "jobs." Because they did not come in and dry-clean my uniform when I could not, I was summoned to a very embarrassing meeting with my very awkward tour-guide manager, who told me that I smelled bad. To make matters worse, I had to tell it like a funny story when my friends asked what had happened, though I was secretly shamed.

— "Sarah Walker"

This is a momentous occasion. Whether your child's first job comes at age twenty–one or twenty–eight, you should be extremely proud of them. Sure, when they were in school, they had summer jobs as camp counselors or selling weed, but this is the real thing! Here are some tips that you should follow, as well as pass along to them, on how to help them succeed at their first job.

1. On their first day of work, make sure to pack them a healthy bag lunch and maybe include a little note that says how proud you are of them. Attached to this note should be a twenty-dollar bill so that they may go out to happy-hour drinks with the new friends they make at work. If they don't live at home anymore, FedEx has a very reliable overnight delivery system that will allow the sandwich meats to stay fresh. Have it delivered to their place of work so that they may look very cool and important for having received a package on their very first day! However, please use a pseudonym on the actual package—you don't want people at work to think that your child is a loser for having their parent pack their lunch. A celebrity name would be best. For example, have the package read, "With love, Forest Whitaker," or "I'm so proud of you, Reese Witherspoon." If you are indeed actually Forest Whitaker or Reese Witherspoon, you should visit your child at work and then they'll have tons of friends, though they all probably just want to sleep with you, Forest/Reese.

2. Obviously, your child has to make a good impression at their first job, which means looking good. No one cares about their personality when they first walk in. They just want to gauge if they are attractive enough to warrant respect. Therefore, a first-day or first-job check is in order, around the area of a cool two grand, give or take inflation rates, or international exchange rates if your child is working in another country. This will cover a new suit, new shoes, and a hair-and-makeup team. Wait, I bet a hair-and-makeup team will cost more—

better make that three grand just to be safe. This may be more than your child will make in a month of working at their new job, but they will surely receive a huge raise based on their stunning good looks. Be sure to hammer in this point to your child of looking as attractive as possible. They could also get a great nickname out of it, like "Legs" or "Torso."

3. Remind them that it is okay to flirt with their married boss, but perhaps not the best idea to sleep with them. You'll have to tell them this in a very delicate manner, as obviously all mention of sex to your adult child is strictly off limits, so you may have to speak to them in code. For example, you could say, "Sometimes it's best to gaze at the shiny apple instead of picking it—we all know what happened to Eve," and then give them a long, knowing wink. I assure you that your child will totally understand this biblical allusion to be equated with forbidden boss sex and will be extremely grateful that you were not more explicit, though they might be slightly creeped out by the wink, which, nonetheless, is necessary.

4. You should be very explicit when telling them not to get wasted at office parties, specifically office Christmas parties, mostly because that would be sooooo cliché and verrrrry eighties of them. Remind them that an open bar is a very, *very* dangerous thing, and goes hand in hand with the previous tip about Eve and the forbidden apple and whatnot. Also, what with digital cameras and the Internet, drunken pictures of them close-talking to their boss and then falling into a tray of tiny sandwiches may not be the best thing to be circulating around when they are on their job search after being shit-canned post-Christmas-party.

5. However, as a corollary to the above rule, if they are going to drink on a work night (without their co-workers or boss), they should not go to sleep and should just keep drinking, because being drunk at work will make them a lot more likable than being hung over at work. People will marvel at their witty conversational skills and overall ebullient personality. Just make sure that they shower thoroughly and take Listerine strips. (Chewing gum is tacky.)

6. Make sure that they have a readily available arsenal of pop-culture references and are adequately caught up on the latest sitcoms and *Gilmore Girls* episodes for idle friend-making chatter. Yes, everyone quotes *Caddyshack* and *Old School*. But this is for investment banking and/or trader douchebags, which your child hopefully isn't. That is, if they're in investment banking or trading, hopefully they aren't a douchebag (doubtful, I'm sorry to say). Anyway, if they really want to be popular, they should exclusively quote *Ghostbusters* and *Ghostbusters II*. It'll be their "thing."

HELPING YOUR CHILD GET A JOB
Only Bitter People Hate Nepotism

My parents are directly responsible for my current job, which is writing a book. They didn't get me the book deal—they are both lawyers—but they provide endless inspiration. I won't tell you what the book is about, but I couldn't have written it without them.

— "S.W.W."

If you're a successful professional in the same field that your child wants to enter or you have some sweet connections in the exact place where your child wants to work, that is awesome. There is no shame in using your clout to help your child get a job, unless your child has some sort of sense of honor or wants to do it on their own, then you can let them have their "pride" or whatever. However, if you want to put in a good word with your old college roomie, Tick-Tock, go right ahead. You have a good kid, and after they get a little push from you, they can make their own way. Tick-Tock will treat them like any other employee, but will often want to talk about your college days, which your child will have to tolerate even though they find it extremely annoying. It's like, Live in the now, Tick-Tock!

That is as far as you should go, though. Putting in a good word is one thing, actively creating your child's résumé, making phone calls to potential employers for them, setting up interviews, even *going* on these interviews, is completely out of the question. Many of you may deem this unthinkable, but believe you me, many parents actually take this actively inappropriate role in their children's lives. They wrote their children's college-admission essays, edited their term papers, and now they accompany them to job fairs and try to sit in on interviews.

Right now everyone should be gasping. That is, assuming there is a group of you reading this at the same time, over each other's shoulder, and punching each other in disbelief. If you're reading this alone, only you should be gasping, and maybe you should slap yourself across the face to make sure that you're not dreaming.

But it's true! How ridiculous is that? Some parents actually think that it's best for their child if they never let them deal with their own life, always having a hand in their every move. I believe the term is "helicopter parents," and I see how that would make sense, but it implies something far cooler, like they are half-person half-helicopter and are blessed with the ability to fly, or at least to hover. It is quite the opposite. I prefer to call them "Overbearing Parents," as it is much more to the point and implies nothing remotely cool at all ... except for bears. But bears are more scary than cool and could tear you limb from limb, much like Overbearing Parents. Listen, my own mother is an Overbearing Parent. Once, when I was a junior in high school, she called up my ceramics teacher to protest my well-deserved B instead of an A, which would have been very clearly undeserved. I tried to tell her not to, but she was intent on sticking up for me, in that she wanted me to get into a good college. So, she had the best intentions, but ultimately the teacher hated me, and rightly so. But that was the extent of her Overbearing Parent–ness, and she learned to let me take care of myself, and I have learned that if I ever take an adult-education ceramics class, I will not be such a slacker and will make that pinch pot in the allotted amount of time.

If you're an Overbearing Parent, let's have a one-on-one convo, right now. Pretend like I'm doing that hand gesture where I put two fingers to my eyes and then point them at your eyes. Yeah, that's how serious I am about this conversation right now. Since I can't hear you, I'll make up your dialogue as I assume you would respond. I will play the role of myself. You shall play the role of Overbearing Parent (OBP).

ME: You have to stop being an Overbearing Parent! You must trust your child enough that they can live their own life with the tools you've given them.

OBP: *I'm a crazy parent! Call me crarent!*

ME: No, I will not, and, no, you're not crazy. You're just being a bit overbearing. There's still time to back off and let your child find their own way. They are, after all, an adult.

OBP: *Sometimes I eat nothing but cranberries!*

ME: Well, that can't be too healthy. Listen, to get back on point, I know it's tough to acknowledge that your child will have to go it alone in the harsh real world, but they will only gain success if they learn through failure and their own experiences.

OBP: *I can hear the ocean in my shoe!*

ME: Hey, that's a good idea. Maybe it's time you took a vacation. You know you're just stressing yourself out by taking on your child's responsibilities.

OBP: *I like the smell of burning hair!*

ME: I'm afraid that you're losing perspective on what actual parenting is. The point is to do as much as you can until your child leaves home and then to provide support, but let them lead their own life. You're not do-ing them any favors by doing everything for them.

OBP: *Want to hear my Ray Charles impression? La la la la!*

ME: That sounds nothing like Ray Charles. You were just yelling "La." Listen, I want you to talk with your child and say that you've decided to give them space to find their own job and apartment and whatever else arises. I can guarantee you that they'll be grateful, even relieved.

OBP: *I am crarent, hear me roar! Raaaaaaaaaaarrrrrrrrrr!!!*

ME: I'm glad we had this talk.

Well, that was certainly an informative conversation. I think it is appropriate to drop the term "Overbearing Parent" and adopt the moniker "Crarent" for these types of parents. It's pithy and sounds like a type of delicious dried fruit. Also, the Crarents thought of it themselves, so they may take full ownership of it and not be offended.

I've just gotten word that the Crarents are offended, and by "Crarents" I mean "my mother." I've agreed to let her tell her side of the story, as she believes that her call to my ceramics teacher in high school was simply good parenting. Okay, Mom, you have the floor. Just don't totally embarrass me and have everyone stop reading. And if you could type at least three hundred words, that would be super helpful.

A MEMO FROM LINDA WALKER
Mother to Sarah Walker, and Non-crarent

Hello, everyone. I'm not used to writing in this type of format. I'm far more comfortable with legal briefs, which I write quite frequently so that I may support my children, specifically, Sarah, as she writes a book about how her parents mucked her up and continue to do so. Except she doesn't use the word "mucked," now does she? She prefers to be vulgar. She certainly did not learn that language from me. She probably picked it up at one of the many taverns she frequents. I happen to know that she once dated an Army man that she picked up in one of these taverns. I don't even want to know what she learned from him. Oh, please don't misunderstand me. I appreciate the irony of writing a book complaining about one's parents as one types on a brushed-steel $3,000 Mac laptop that my hundred-hour workweeks bought for a certain someone. Anyway, as far as the ceramics incident goes, I called up Sarah's ceramics teacher Sarah's *senior* year of high school, as opposed to her junior year. This seems to have slipped Sarah's mind conveniently, as she has failed to remember that she came down with a case of senioritis that rendered her unable to fulfill her pinch-pot requirements in the slacker-hippie class she thought she could just coast through and have an easy A on her transcript, which might do something to offset the C+ she received in Pre-Calculus her junior year. Sarah tearfully complained to me that her teacher was being unfair, and that having a B on her transcript would seriously impede her from getting into the college of her choice. So, at *Sarah's request*, I made a call to her art teacher, who calmly explained to me that as Sarah had not completed one of her assignments, she could only but give her a B, and that was being generous. When I informed Sarah of my call, she yelled at me for making her look like a spoiled brat in front of her teacher. Like she needed any help from me. Did I mention that on one of her college applications, when asked if she had visited the school, which was about a ten-minute drive from our home, Sarah checked "no"? It's no wonder she was rejected from her safety. But now, because of that one incident, I'm a "Crarent." Well, let me tell you something, Miss I'm Writing a Book About How My Parents Mucked Me Up—

Okay, thanks, Mom!

Wow, it's amazing how different people have different perspectives on history. It's interesting how this happens in both our political and social consciousnesses. I guess history is written by those who write it, and I'm writing this book, not my mother. By the way, I have a new, adorable name for my mom! She can be called "Crom"! It sounds like something a bird would screech. When it's angry and not thinking rationally about how things actually happened. *Crom! Crom!* Anyway, thanks, Crom!

A MEMO FROM LINDA WALKER: MY NAME IS NOT CROM

My daughter, it seems, has thought up a cute little nickname for me: "Crom." However, my name is not Crom, it is Linda Walker. I find it incredibly disrespectful that she would find it appropriate to call me "Crazy Mom" after all I have done for her. What if I started calling her Crarah? Hey, everybody, it's Crazy Sarah! Let's call her Crarah! How would she like that? Not at all, I'm sure. And I'm seriously considering not placing the phone call she asked me to make to her neighbor who sometimes makes soup that smells weird and gives her nightmares. You can just go ahead and have those nightmares, Sarah. See what I care. Okay, fine, I'll make the call, but I will not be referred to as Crom!

A MESSAGE FROM THE AUTHOR TO CROM

Dear Crom,

I never said that "Crom" stood for "Crazy Mom." I should have specified. Actually, it stands for "Crikey, Mom!" As in, "Crikey, Mom, you've done so much for me!" Also, Crarah does not have the same ring as "Crarent" or "Crom." I'm sorry, it just doesn't roll off the tongue. Anyway, let's put these differences behind us. I am just trying to find an equilibrium for our parent-child relationship and help others along the way. So if you could, for, like, two seconds, stay out of my business, I would really appreciate that. Well, stay out of my business *after* you make that call to my neighbor. I think it's a curry soup or something. Thank you, Crom.

Sincerely,
Sarah

A MESSAGE FROM THE AUTHOR TO EVERYONE BESIDES CROM

It appears as though my mother has cut me off. Well. That's just great. If this book suffers for it, because I can't afford enough Diet Coke to keep me properly hydrated and alert after I suffer from sleep deprivation because of my inhalation-of-curry-soup-caused nightmares, you know whom to blame. However, as I am a selfless person, I will soldier on, despite certain hardships ahead.

Believe it or not, this book is not my first foray into philanthropy. I have for a long time lent my talents and support to other organizations and peoples who need my help. I would like to provide you now with my résumé of philanthropic work.

YMCA
West Hartford, Connecticut, 1986–1987
When I was six, I participated in a youth basketball league in which I shot at hoops that were six feet high (as opposed to the ten-foot regulation height) and I never complained. A complaint would have surely shut down the YMCA, depriving many children of after-school activities, so I effectively saved the YMCA of West Hartford at age six.

Berkley Ballroom Dancing School
Hartford, Connecticut, 1993–1994
At age twelve I was enrolled in ballroom-dancing classes where I learned such steps as the fox trot, the waltz, and the cha-cha-cha. I danced with boys who were much shorter than myself, which made them incredibly un-comfortable, and I made them feel this acutely, telling them repeatedly to stop staring at my rack[1], which they couldn't help but do, their eyes being at rack level. They carried this lesson of humility with them, so that when they were grown they harkened back to those days of ballroom-dancing shame whenever they were about to be a jerk to a girl. This resulted in many boys in the Hartford area being very respectful to girls. As a result, a majority of girls bypassed the horrible self-conscious-ness that comes as a result of boy jerkiness. This led them to succeed in school and win a collective eight Pulitzer Prizes and three Peabody Awards.

Mites Soccer Team Coach
West Hartford, Connecticut, 1998–1999
As a senior in high school I coached tiny five-year-olds in the art of soccer. Tiny five-year-olds play soccer with a pack mentality, with no regard for spacing or strat-egy. It's quite adorable to see twenty little kids franti-cally move from one side of the field to the other as one … until you realize that that is no way to play soc-cer and if they continue to move as a pack they will never have a sense of individuality. So, I started a series

---

[1] I didn't exactly have a rack at the time, but it was funny to say "rack."
For the record, I now have a fantastic rack.

of rumors about each of the children that turned them against each other ("Lila says that Matty smells"), and this lead them to want to stay far away from each other, especially Matty, since everyone thought that he smelled. As a result, we had the best spacing of the entire league and went on to win at least two more games than we had anticipated. Yes, no one was in a celebratory mood because they had all been turned against each other, but the important thing is that we won and the kids learned to look out for number one.

Lip-Synch Contest
Amherst College, Amherst, Massachusetts, April 2002
My junior year at Amherst, my roommates and I participated in the third annual "Room Draw Lip-Synch Contest," the winner of which would receive first pick for room draw. My seven other roommates and myself choreographed a complicated dance to a montage of *Grease* songs. It was excellent in its professionalism, originality, and general playfulness. However, we lost out to a bunch of boys dressed in drag grinding to whatever J.Lo song was popular at the time. I wrote a stinging article to the *Amherst Student* in which I ironically suggested that the only way to win a lip-synch contest is to be creative—that is, to dress like a man—and then I ended on this zinger: "After all, a number-one pick in room draw doesn't come with just a little song and dance." This article caused a frank intra-college debate, not about the norms of gender equality and creativity but about how fucking stupid it is to write an op-ed article based on a lip-synch contest and how annoying the *Grease* soundtrack is. As a result, op-ed

articles to the *Amherst Student* are now carefully screened and the music of *Grease* is banned from the room-draw lip-synch contest.

Soup Kitchen
New York, New York, December 2005
I signed up to volunteer on Christmas Eve at a soup kitchen in Hell's Kitchen and very much considered going, but then I realized that it was Christmas Eve and that I could be out to dinner with my friends, and not with totally depressing homeless people. Then I realized that it was the season of giving and I put on my coat to go. Then I realized that homeless people need soup every day, not just on Christmas Eve, so I could easily go on a random Tuesday night in January or something. This made me feel much better, because then I wouldn't be one of those people whose conscience just pricks at them during the holidays. I am socially conscious at all times. I have thought about going to that soup kitchen on nonholiday days and this makes me feel like I am really socially aware. So, the other day, I made a bowl of cream-of-mushroom soup and gave it to the first person I saw on the street, who may or may not have been homeless, but the point is, they were surprised. And everyone likes surprises.

Eleventh Street
New York, New York, July 2006
I intercepted a group of international tourists who were on the *Sex and the City* tour in the West Village and explained to them that simply going on the tour will not make them have the lives of the women on the show,

and that they wouldn't want them anyway, and that, moreover, eating a lot of cupcakes at the Magnolia Bakery, which is a stop on the tour, will not make you a size 0 Sarah Jessica Parker. They seemed to understand, as they repeatedly called me "Puta," which I believe means "Saint" in Spanish.

THE GIFT OF TECHNOLOGY
Helping Your Child Through
Their Stay-at-Home Twenties

Perhaps you have forgotten, because you were too busy working hard and doing whatever you crazy kids did back in the day, but one's twenties are a very difficult time, rife with the anxiety of knowing that one will not fully appreciate how awesome and young one is and how much fun one is having until it is too late. Are you okay? I thought I just saw you wipe away a tear. No? Anyway, you must provide your child with a safe environment to contemplate these subjects. Internet access and full cable service, including HBO On Demand, are also helpful. Your child must make a complete inventory of all that is out there in the world so that they may make an informed decision of where to go when they leave home. The World Wide Web and the plethora of movies and original series provided by HBO On Demand will provide them with all the secondhand information they need know. For example, if provided with HBO services, they will discover, before it is too late and they decide to move there without knowing what they are getting into, that New Jersey is full of mobsters and crime and that New York is replete with loose women who employ bad puns to explain away their sexual indiscretions. Therefore, obviously, steer your child away from ultimately living in New Jersey or New York. Hell, let's throw in Connecticut, too, and make it the whole tristate area. The Nutmeg State? Let's be serious: What is Connecticut hiding?

LET'S GO ONLINE! SOCIALLY!

Online social networks, which they will inevitably join as a result of unlimited Internet usage, as accessed by a wireless network on a new laptop so as to allow easy movement throughout the house (what if it's cold in the den and sunny in the living room? do you want your child to be alone in the cold dark on the Internet? that's depressing), will allow them to build a cadre of friends. Online friendships are the best kind of friendships in that they can be accessed in seconds and similarly denied with a click of a button. Your child might even simulate the experience of having a boyfriend or girlfriend, and you may rest easy knowing that their online sexual experiences carry no risk of disease and will not be a burden to your health insurance, which your child still shares with you. I mean, if they still live at home it stands to reason that you would provide them with health insurance as well. What are you, some sort of monster who would deny your child the basic human right of health?

I thought not.

You've no doubt heard of online social networks. If you've read the newspaper, a magazine, or watched TV over the past couple of years, you've seen endless hard-hitting pieces on them, about why they are so popular with the kids and pedophiles alike. They are where your child probably spends most of their time during the day when they are supposed to be working, and they are 90 percent responsible for the slow atrophy of your child's brain, and limited memory retention.

By the way, the word "social" is not used ironically in "Online Social Networks," even though the first time you heard the phrase and realized that it is primarily a solitary activity you said it like "Online *Social???* Networks." Well, Mr./Ms. Cynical, some of my best friendships were made online. Which reminds me, I have to check one of my four profiles. Deadline schmedline, that dude who's a drummer in Brooklyn might have written me back and I want to see if that hot bartender has a profile.

Three hours later ...

What was I talking about? Oh, yeah. Okay. So, like, here is a brief explanation/overview of the three most popular online social networking sites, which will probably be obsolete by the time this book is published, as the publishing date has been pushed back due to my lack of concentration because of my obsession with these fucking networks.

THE FUCKING NETWORKS

Each online network shares the same basic layout. By simply providing the host with your e-mail address and a password, blood sample, and retinal scan, you are allotted a page in the network, which is your profile. On this profile you post a hot/ironic/ironically hot picture of yourself and then fill out a short questionnaire highlighting your interests, heroes, favorite books, movies, and music. Also, there is the question of relationship status. If you don't want random creepy people writing you, you say that you're in a relationship. If random creepy people hitting on you via the Internet increases your self worth, then you say that you're single. Actually, either way, random creepy people are going to hit on you, so deal with it. However, if you actually make a profile at your age, you are automatically a random creepy person, so you should go ahead and not do that. However, if a random creepy person hits on another random creepy person, the creepiness is negated.

The three most popular (at publishing date) online social networks are Facebook, MySpace, and Friendster. There are others, such as aSmallworld.com, which is reserved for European jet-setting cokeheads, who presumably have time to go online between Gstaad and South Hampton. Unfortunately, I am not one of these jet-setting cokeheads (give it time, someday), so I do not have access, but I assume it is made of diamonds and that, even though the Internet is usually safe for sexual encounters, one would automatically contract a high-class STD.

Friendster

I can almost guarantee you that Friendster is obsolete right now, as at the time of writing, it is severely uncool.

I asked my thirteen-year-old cousin about it the other day and she didn't know what it was. She was even abandoning MySpace to go to Facebook. However, kids these days love irony, so maybe its very uncoolness will spawn its comeback, as Myspace is certain to jump the shark anytime now, as thirteen-year-olds seem to be the taste-makers nowadays. As a side note, a friend of mine noted that the phrase "jump the shark" has itself "jumped the shark." Did your brain just explode? Mine did when he mentioned this to me. So, he suggested that we rename the phrase "jump the shark" to "Roseanne won the lottery," which makes more sense anyway. No? Oh, well, "Roseanne won the lottery" refers to the seminal eighties and nineties sitcom *Roseanne*, starring Roseanne Barr as a mother to a lower-middle-class family in Illinois. Had Roseanne ever won the lottery, she would not have had to work at her job as a waitress nor would her family have ever struggled, which provides much of the comedy and heart of the show.

What was I talking about? Right. Friendster.

Friendster is the network that started it all, and was immediately cool with the hipster set, and although I would get random e-mail after random e-mail saying that someone had invited me to be their Friendster, I would refuse on the basis of the pure idiocy of the name and concept, as I am a far thinker and can anticipate trends with an oracle-like sense. Yes, I was wrong, Friendster was a huge hit, but that doesn't make it any less idiotic. The one good thing about Friendster is that it lists your friends in alphabetical order, unlike MySpace, which is too cool to obey the rules of the alphabet and if you want to find a friend you have to sift through *literally hundreds of profiles, because, yes, I have hundreds of friends*.

One of the main benefits of these networks is that you can anonymously view the profiles of crushes, ex-significant-others, and the people they are currently dating. Yes, one could roam profiles freely and indiscriminately, often checking back to one's ex-significant-other's profile several time a day/hour. However, one day, without warning, Friendster lifted the veil of anonymity and one could see who had viewed one's profile within the past month. Needless to say, many of us were screwed, caught, "had," as it were, by Friendster, and the subsequent embarrassment was not even alleviated by seeing the people who had viewed your profile, as you now empathized with these people, as you had been caught in a similar manner. This embarrassment has only now started to fade, though writing this now brings back painful memories of online-stalking that one-night stand, who surely saw that I had checked his profile many a time. I'm going to check it again right now, actually. Do not fear! Now one may click a box that says, "View profile anonymously." Perhaps Friendster was trying to teach us all a subtle lesson in taking responsibility for your actions, but to Friendster I say, "You're an inanimate online social network in no position to teach lessons, so shut up!"

MySpace

Before I get into a description of MySpace, let me just say that much has been done by way of MySpace in the form of parody. I am not trying to follow in the illustrious footsteps of so many teenagers from Michigan or whatever who make MySpace spoof movies or deconstruct the types of poses and angles in MySpace photos. I simply want to make more clear to you, the parent, your child's Internet drug of choice. And since that Internet drug of choice is porn, I choose instead to make more clear their second Internet drug of choice, MySpace. So here I go.

MySpace started off primarily as a way for bands to promote their music. Many people use it for personal profiles, much like Friendster, but MySpace is much more popular. Now, in addition to bands and personal profiles, there are specific pages for comedy, film, and books. (You should be this book's MySpace friend.) Usually, you get many requests a day to be a random band's friend. A band's profile usually has about four of their songs that you can listen to, sometimes even download for free. There is also the option to add a band's song to your profile so that the song plays when someone clicks on your profile. The song you add either shows how cool you are (for example, Morrissey's new single), how funny you are (the theme song from *The NeverEnding Story*), or how *super* cool you are if you don't add a song, which says, "I know so much about music, there is really no point in trying to encompass my vast knowledge in one song." Then that person lights a cigarette and spits angrily.

There are four types of bands on MySpace:

1. The band that was already established before MySpace (BM) and probably never checks their profile, but they

have 874,092 friends because they are so awesome. Some of their songs are featured on their site, but they are not available for download.

2. The really great indie band from Brooklyn/Akron/Sheffield that is just dying for you to hear their music and will let you download it for free because they are just so fucking pure and good. They have a hot lead singer/guitarist who is underage, *or* they are in, like, their thirties because they've been paying their dues and perfecting their craft or whatever.

3. A sixteen-year-old from Spokane, Washington, whose music sucks. I mean, really, really sucks. And they individually message you to be your friend and practically force their music on you. But they've got spunk, I'll give them that.

4. Who the fuck are these people? Please do not try to befriend me. You frighten and confuse me with your alt/country/hip-hop/heavy-metal genre.

Whatever type of band or musician wants to befriend you, you'll probably say yes, because, ultimately, it's just a numbers game. There is a direct relationship between how cool you are and the number of friends you have. *Unless*, oh, unless you've been signed up for MySpace for a couple of years and insist on only having twelve friends. Then you're badass!! You don't need anyone! You are so alone, so very alone.

Facebook

Facebook was started by a Harvard student, exclusively for college students, and has now expanded to high school. The creator is now selling it, or has sold it, for about a billion dollars. If you are not the parents of this child, you have failed. If you are the parents of this child, give yourselves a pat on the back. Literally. You deserve a trophy. A billion-dollar trophy. Maybe this isn't the best way to spend your son's billions, but who else in the world would have a *billion-dollar* trophy? No one. Just you. It would be made of pink diamonds and leather made from the skin of an endangered species. You'll keep it in a specially constructed hall of mirrors so it looks like you have an infinite number of billion-dollar trophies. But when people ask you where you keep your billion-dollar trophy, you can say, "Oh, in the bathroom!" like you're Tom Hanks or something.

Facebook.com bears with it a sense of elitism that Friendster and MySpace do not have, as one must have a college e-mail address to access it. Also, it categorizes you by school, and shows the number of friends you have at different schools. So, if on your profile I see that you have twenty-five Facebook friends who go/went to Harvard, and one who goes to Manchester Community Technical College, I can safely assume that you are a snobbish bastard who, in a fit of conscience, decided to accept your childhood best friend, who you haven't spoken to for ten years, as your Facebook friend. Wow, good for you. They are, after all, just trying to scrape by on two jobs to get themselves a college education so they can provide, for their infant child and new spouse, the life that was denied them. I'm glad that you can sometimes keep them in your thoughts when you sign into Facebook. Dick.

THE PROFILE

Meeting interesting people with similar interests actually comes second on these online social networks. The primary goal is to make one's profile, and therefore oneself, look as cool as possible. Usually this means writing a comprehensive list of movies, books, and bands that one probably likes but also some are for show. Who *really* loves the *Cremaster* cycle? You? Well, you're a pretentious asshole. Maybe for another person, showing how awesome they are means posting pictures of them with hot women and, under "Occupation," writing, "Playa." This is their prerogative, obviously. However, there is just no way that I, for example, would write back to them if they wrote me a message that maybe said, "'Sup babygrl? A mutual friend told me to write to you …" Let me just say that I am positive that we have no mutual fri— Oh. You know Todd? Todd from Michigan? Oh. Okay. Well, thanks, Todd.

THE FRIEND COMMENTS

All of these sites have options for friends to write on your profile in a designated space. On Friendster, it's called a "Testimonial," on MySpace it's called a "Comment," and on Facebook you write on someone's "Wall." Each gives the opportunity for unbridled voyeurism. People post private conversations for all to see, when they really could just write them an e-mail. But people need to know that they are friends and are befriended alike, also that they are super funny and cool. In this respect, Friendster probably makes the most sense, as the word "Testimonial" implies that you are writing about this person for others to see, so the entire world can see what a fucking cool dude this person is. However, on MySpace comments and the Facebook wall, all you're saying is that you know that other people are reading this private exchange between you and this person and that you hope they like it. It's like talking too loudly on your cell phone while you are telling your friend that you saw Ryan Gosling last night at a bar and he totally looked in your direction, but whatever, no big deal, celebrities are people, too.

I could show you an example of a specific MySpace profile by cutting and pasting my own. But I don't want to. The awesome nature of my profile might be too much for you to handle and you may get the urge to create your own profile so that you might immediately befriend me. This would be disastrous. Now go sit in a darkened, computer-free room with a glass of brandy to calm yourself. It's not worth it.

Technology That You Should Never Learn

1. TEXT MESSAGING: If your child's best friend, whom they trust the most in the world, can mind-fuck them with text messaging ("Come to party! HE's here! JK. Or am I?"), imagine the damage that you could do.

2. ONLINE PROFILES: I realize that there is an entire section dedicated to these, but you must never *ever* create one for yourself, to either meet new people or spy on your child.

3. INSTANT MESSAGING: This immediate and direct access to your child when they are at home or at work is unnerving. Your child likes it when people aren't too accessible—it makes them more attractive. Try that tactic out. I bet they'll want to talk to you more and maybe even drunk-dial you inappropriately if you act aloof.

4. BLOCKING CALLER ID: Your child must *always* be able to identify you if you call and screen you as required, like if they're in the middle of hooking up or something.[1]

Technology That You Really Should Have Learned By Now

1. RECORDING A SHOW ON A VCR: Well, it's too late now. But it would have been helpful back in the nineties when your child really wanted to see that episode of *Saturday Night Live* that Macaulay Culkin hosted.

2. DVR/TIVO: Now you can redeem yourself by DVR/ TiVo'ing all of your child's favorite shows, so that when they return home they have an entertainment lineup that will make their visit even *more* delightful, by providing an escape into the wonderful world of television.

3. COMPUTERS: Seriously, how do you not know how to use a computer by now? I swear to you that iTunes is exceptionally easy to operate. You don't need to make

---

[1] Actually, no one should answer the phone, no matter who is calling, if they are in the middle of hooking up. My friend did this to me once when I called and she was obviously midcoitus, and it grossed me out to no end. I gave her some stern words, not that she cared, as she was getting laid.

your child load all of your Barry Manilow CDs onto iTunes when they're home for the holidays. They have better things to do, like watch the shows that you DVR'd for them.

4. CELL PHONES (EXCEPTING TEXT MESSAGING): Again, cell phones are not hard to figure out. Twelve-year-olds have them these days. It's just a tiny phone that's not connected to a cord. That's the only difference between a cell and your twenty-pound rotary phone.

PARTYING WITH YOUR CHILD
The Party's Over Before It's Begun

I came home to visit my parents on a random weekend and my dad caught me smoking a joint out of my window in my room. Instead of being angry with me, he asked if he could have a drag, except he said "toke," which made me die a little. But, rather than get in trouble, I let him have some. Half an hour later he was telling me his philosophy on how human beings are not meant to be monogamous, and if he could be any animal, he would be a bonobo. Then he got paranoid that Mom would find us and insisted on spending the next three hours in my room. It was the longest three hours of my life.

— *"Walker"*

Partying with your child is a terrible, terrible idea. Although your relationship is strained after several months/years/decades of living at home and alcohol/drugs seem like the most obvious and effective social lubricant—after all, it works at the office picnic like a charm (or so you think)—you would be horribly mistaken. In any conversation, when alcohol and drugs come into play, painful truths and long-buried emotions rise to the surface in some sort of sordid tableau.[1] Sometimes this can be a long-over-due cleansing experience, but that only applies to ex-lovers and conversations with a mirror.

Now, obviously there is a difference between drinking with your child and doing drugs with your child. "Drugs," in this case, means marijuana. Anything else is so crazy fucked up, it's the stuff of fake memoirs. So, unless you're a fictional teenage Southern mom who turns tricks at the truck stop to support your fictional transgendered son, you have no excuse to be smoking anything other than weed (if that) with your child. Oh, yes, smoking weed with your child may seem like a funny, edgy idea at the time, especially if you're on vacation in Hawaii and relaxed and feeling young or something and your child is actively urging you on (probably because they are already high), but, again, you would be horribly mistaken.

A necessary distinction is that it is perfectly acceptable for your child to drink, just as it is perfectly acceptable for you to drink, but these two acts are only acceptable if they are carried out separately. It's clearly cooler for your child to drink, especially with friends at their favorite local dive bar where they make revelatory comments about life and love and lasting friendships, which they will then scrawl onto cocktail napkins with the idea of turning them into a screenplay, only they won't be able to read them the next day. It's okay, they weren't that good anyway. With you, if you're at the same local

---

[1] Not like an elegantly painted baroque bacchanal scene with naked nymphs committing bestiality with well-muscled, wine-soaked centaurs, more like a terribly rendered velvet painting meant to represent feelings and smelling of Franzia.

dive bar, you're just a creepy older man who people look at and wonder why you're not at home. These people who are looking at you are probably your child and their friends, which is very embarrassing for your child, who cannot even pretend not to know you, since they are sitting with their friends from high school who know you as the parent who screamed bad ideas at all of the basketball games. (One does not set a pick when one is on defense.) Hell, you could be a creepy older woman, too. Chances are, however, if you're a woman, you're getting hammered over a bottle of Pinot Gris with the other suburban moms, sitting in a big kitchen around an Italian-marble island with a bunch of never-used copper pots hanging over it. Either way, your binge drinking lacks the luster of youth, the ultimate mask of depression. Still, drink away, Drunky! There are probably a lot of things you don't want to think about, like how your twenty-five-year-old lives with posters of the German industrial metal band Rammstein on his wall, so why deprive yourself of that great happiness maker, Delusion? You are great, yes, you are! And you know what? Everyone here is great. Round of drinks, on you! Let's all hug. Too much hug, get off of me! Sorry, that was the alcohol talking.

If you are dating someone, and you are going to take your new significant other out in public with your child, it is your duty that they behave responsibly. This includes not getting too drunk at dinner and/or criticizing anything that your child does, especially if it's something creative like a play that they wrote or something that you all just went to see performed. If your drunk significant other says something like "I didn't like the ending of your play" to your child while chugging a Pilsner, you must immediately chloroform your date so that there may be no more disturbances such as this one. One can purchase chloroform at a good rate at any local spy supply store, turpentine serves well as an alternate, and all you need is a clean handkerchief to apply it. Don't use too much—you just want to take them out of the conversation for a while.

Drugswise, it is not only perfectly acceptable but also super cool for your child to do drugs. This is not meant facetiously. Any pothead will tell you that weed has never killed a person, whereas tobacco has killed millions. There being no marijuana-related deaths is an arguable point, granted, but surely your child is safe at home or at a friend's house whilst consuming mind-altering substances, and not going through a fast-food drive-through while an adorable little girl riding a pink bicycle inexplicably pedals directly in front of the car.

As far as cocaine and other drugs go, well, you only live once! Just kidding, your child probably shouldn't be doing those things, unless a rock star/model is pushing a couple of lines in front of their nose and urging them to do it, because then the possibility of hot rocker/model sex is infinitely more probable. Just make sure that their definition of "rock star" is correct. You don't want them to waste hot rocker sex on a bunch of sixteen-year-olds in a faux punk band from Canada who sing about how they like to steal their dads' smokes. Also, remind them to use a condom. Again, just kidding, you should have stopped having those conversations a while ago, though I would hope that you would have raised your child to know that there is a 100 percent chance that the rock star/model in question is disease-ridden. We shall assume that your child probably knows how diseased rockers/models are and will use a condom for the best sex of their life. Anyway, why would you ever be there with them at that coke party? That's just crazy.

You are too old to be having sex, by the way. Therefore, it should go without saying that it's borderline weird for you to be doing drugs. Yes, drugs were cool in the sixties and seventies ... and eighties and nineties. Let's be honest, drugs have always been cool. The drugs haven't changed, you have. Up there on the Depressing Image Scale is the aging hippie smoking weed as their frightened children and scared but slightly amused friends look on.

Confused by this from all the wine you've been drinking/weed you've been smoking/coke you've been snorting? Here is a Venn diagram to summarize these points:

Venn Diagram of Alcohol

Venn Diagram of Drugs

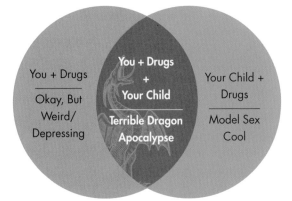

As you can clearly see from the middle portion, or intersection, of the Venn diagram, the merging of You, Your Child, and Alcohol results in a Confrontational Cry-Fighting Apocalypse. Let's say that your child is home for the weekend because they need a break from the city that they live in and going home is the quickest way to realize that they love the city with all of their heart and should never, ever leave. You decide to go to a restaurant in the center of town for dinner, even though your child should have known better and vetoed the idea if they did not want to run into that stoner douchebag kid that they went to high school with who is now working as a waiter at that restaurant.

As you sit down across from one another, you both realize at the exact same moment that this weekend will be the opposite of relaxing and a montage of all the reasons why it was awesome when your child left home (finally) and moved to the city flashes by, sort of like the *Wonder Years* opening credits, only far less happy and old-timey. Instead of "With a Little Help From My Friends" by Joe Cocker serving as the background music, all you can think of is that terrible song "Meet Virginia" by Train, probably because this terrible restaurant is playing it at this very terrible moment. As though you have rehearsed this a thousand times, you simultaneously call the former high-school stoner/douchebag-now-waiter over and order two dirty Grey Goose martinis, straight up with olives. (You are, after all, related and have both always individually considered the dirty martini the classiest of aperitifs.) You down them, perhaps, in retrospect, too quickly, seeing as how stoner/d-bag/waiter (SDW) has not yet left the table and is now looking at you both, gape-mouthed. Be that as it may, you both feel much better, and maybe SDW could exercise some class and close his mouth and get you both another martini. Hell, you should probably get a bottle of wine with dinner. After all, it's been a while, hasn't it? You guys have a lot to talk about! Cut to the aforementioned Cry-Fighting Apocalypse, as seen in the intersection of the Drinking Venn diagram. This involves glasses being broken and staid suburbanites looking on in horror as they witness uncontrollable sobbing and girlish slapping on the part of both you and your child, which is ultimately directed toward your SDW, who tries to break up the fight, and who, if he weren't so high, would know to stay the hell out of your business. Ironically, however, this is the most altruistic move SDW will ever make, however unwittingly, because you and your child join forces against him, laying aside your grievances against each other. Afterward, you will come to view this as a bonding moment and will recall it with fondness: "Remember when we told that SDW what was what? No one messes with us! (*High-five.*)" Only years later will it occur to you that being mean to the wait staff, however douchey they may be, is always unacceptable, and you will be shamed by this knowledge and know that it would have never occurred had you just laid off the booze.

LET'S KEEP IT IN THE FAMILY
Partying With Your Child's Friends

I hosted a party at my house over Thanksgiving and a bunch of my friends from home came over and we started to play drinking games. My father decided to join in on the fun and before long he was playing beer pong against my best friend and called him a "pussy." This was especially distressful for my best friend, as his mother had called his father a pussy right before she walked out on the family. I felt awkward about it and let him win the next beer-pong game, which I guess was ultimately a mistake, since this led to much drunken crying about his family later in the night. What a pussy.

— "Walker"

There are worse scenarios, believe it or not, than the aforementioned. For example, it's worse when your drunken antics reach beyond the sphere of your child and a single waiter, to a slew of your child's friends, who have come over for an impromptu party. Perhaps they are all playing a drinking game, and you think it would be fun to join in. Or you want to act as host, so you pour yourself a fishbowl–sized glass of Gewürztraminer and saunter around the party, trying to appear relevant. Of course, it is your right to be in your own house and hang out if you so choose. After all, they are probably drinking alcohol that you purchased, since, in a bout of high-school nostalgia, your child decided to raid your liquor cabinet. Just keep this rule in mind: Never engage in a drinking game with your child and their friends, especially if said game involves Ping-Pong balls and several full cups of beer. These games, in addition to being conducive to extreme drunkenness, also engage the competitive spirit, and no one wants to see you call your child, your child's friend, or perhaps your child's significant other a "pussy" as they stand across the Ping-Pong table from you. It's weird that you even know to use that word. You may feel the need to bond with your child's friends, and perhaps you ask one of their best friends, whom you have known since they were in fifth grade, about their parents' recent divorce. Perhaps you feel the need to empathize with them in such a manner that demonstrates how heartbroken you are personally by their divorce and how you never saw it coming and how they are both such good people, you just *cannot believe* they could do this after *thirty years* of marriage!

Also, since you have not seen many of your child's friends in a long time and they are now adults, many of them quite good-looking adults, perhaps you feel, under the influence of alcohol, that some playful flirtation is in order. This is perhaps the worst, most heinous act you could ever commit against your child. As you drunkenly leer at one of their closest friends from childhood and make suggestive comments, the secondhand embarrassment of your child's friends is almost palpable and, as the friend does their best to laugh it off, your child can think of nothing else but to take a chair and smash you across the back of the head, knocking you out, but unfortunately you try to break your fall by grabbing onto the object of flirtation's breasts or package. The last things you hear before you black out are the terrified screams from the party guests and your glass of booze smashing dramatically as it hits the floor, shards of glass flying in all directions.

DRINKING GAME RULES

If you are going to engage in drinking games with your child and your child's friends, even though I am explicitly telling you that this is a bad idea, you might as well know how to play them correctly. Here are the guidelines for some of the more popular drinking games, so you don't further embarrass your child when you don't know the rules. However, what this brief overview is mainly meant to do is to keep you off these games, since I'm sure you'll realize after reading their descriptions that you never want to engage in this type of activity with your child.

Beirut

EQUIPMENT: Two Ping-Pong balls, a table about six feet long, plastic cups, beer, maybe a creative team T-shirt, but not required.[1]

---

[1] If you were to create T-shirts, some possible ideas could be "Team We'll Regret This Tomorrow," "Team We're Not Related," and "Team I Don't Know the Person Standing Next to Me If They Do Anything Embarrassing."

RULES: Two teams of two stand on opposite sides of a long table, usually about the size of a Ping-Pong table if it isn't actually a Ping-Pong table. In front of each team are ten plastic cups, lined up in a pyramid shape, like so:

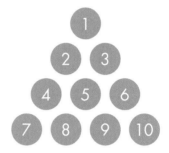

Each cup is about a third or halfway filled up with beer, depending on how shitfaced you want to get. Cheap light beer along the lines of Natural (Natty) Lite, Coors Lite, or Bud Lite is used, as they taste like close to nothing and are easily chugged.

Through a simple two-out-of-three rock-paper-scissors, an arm-wrestling contest, or a cage-match fight to near death, one team is chosen to start the game with both Ping-Pong balls. Each team member shoots the balls at the opposing team's cups, the object being to sink the balls into the cups. If a ball is sunk by a player, the opposing team has to drink the beer in that cup while the team who sunk the ball does some sort of high-five yelling ceremony. Each team gets two shots, unless both team members sink both of their shots, and in that case they get both of the balls back and the other team misses their turn. Each team shoots back and forth, the first team to sink all of the opposing team's cups wins, and the losing team must drink the other team's remaining unsunk cups of beer. Then you will promptly vomit or hit on one of your child's friends. Seriously, don't play this game.

Beer Pong

Similar to Beirut, but Ping-Pong paddles are used instead of simply throwing the ball into the cup. It requires, obviously, more equipment, and it may be argued (by me) that Beirut is the superior game. Again, this is a game that you should not participate in.

Never Have I Ever

This is possibly the worst drinking game you could engage in with your children and their friends, because it's sort of like the truth portion of Truth or Dare but it involves more beer and more embarrassing/raunchy stories. Everyone sits in a circle and one person will say, "Never have I ever …" and say something that they either know that someone in the circle has done or that they have done. If anyone in the circle has done that particular thing, they drink. If only one person drinks, then that person has to tell the story of what they did. So, for example, if someone says, "Never have I ever had a threesome with my neighbor and Javier, the Spanish foreign-exchange student," and your child is the only one to drink, they will have to tell the entire circle how, during the summer of '97, they got drunk off of sangria made by Javier, the Spanish exchange student who was staying with you, and ended up making out with him and the sexy neighbor who was just stopping by to borrow some twine. There's no way you want to hear this story and there's no way your child wants to tell it in front of you, but those are the rules of the game, and the consequences for not telling the story when you are the only one to drink are dire: drinking more. So you can see how your child needs to abide by the rules. Again, never play this game with your child. Never ever.

Kings

The rules of Kings are simple, though many. It just takes some memorizing. A deck of cards is spread in a circle, face down, surrounding a full glass of beer. Everyone sits in a circle around the cards and the beer and, going clockwise, each person picks up a card and follows these rules, which depend on the number or face of the card.

2: *Take*
The person who picked the card takes a sip of beer.

3: *Give*
The person who picked the card makes someone else in the circle drink.

4: *Touch the Floor*
Last person to touch the floor with their hand, drinks. This sounds like an unusually random rule. However, notice that "four" and "floor" rhyme. This rhyming device occurs fre-

quently throughout the game and will prove to be useful for you. Unless a rule doesn't rhyme with its corresponding number and then you're fucked. Usually someone forgets the "four, touch the floor" rule and everyone else in the circle sits around and smirks as the forgetful person innocently looks around and then notices that everyone's hand is on the floor and yells, "Oh, shit!" Hilarity ensues.

5: *Waterfall*

Everyone stands up in a circle and starts drinking their beers at the same time. When the person who picked the card decides to finish, the person to the left of them may stop drinking. When that person decides to stop drinking, the person to the left of them may stop drinking, and so on around the circle. Therefore, the person to the immediate right of the person who picked the card and started the waterfall is the last to stop drinking and hence the most fucked up.

6: *Categories*

The person who picked the card chooses a category. Everyone keeps a steady beat by slapping their hands against their knees and each person, going counterclockwise from the original person, has to say an item from that category, on beat. For example, the category could be "Different ways of saying penis." So, going around the circle to the beat, people would say, "Di-ick!" "Co-ck!" "Johnson!" "Trouser Snake!" The person who can't think of a different name for penis or messes up the beat has to drink. Are you beginning to see why you shouldn't be playing these games?

7: *Chicks*

This is a word used for women. So when someone pulls a seven, the women in the circle, in a ladylike manner, pinkies extended, sip their beers.

8: *Dicks*

Anyone with a dick, that is, the men in the circle, fucking chug their brewskies. Please do not eagerly yell "Dicks!" when an eight comes up and then try to high-five the closest person to you. That will be very embarrassing for both you (in the morning) and your child (at that exact moment).

9: *Bust a Rhyme*

The person who picks the card starts a sentence and the person to their left has to continue it by rhyming. No word may be repeated. If one is, that person drinks. The person who starts the rhyming shouldn't be an idiot and start a sentence with "My sweater is orange" or "I prefer gold to silver." If they do, then they drink, obviously.

10: *Social*

Everyone stands up, cheers, circles their beer once around their head, and drinks. They circle their beers around their heads for no particular reason. I suppose it signifies that the entire circle is drinking.

JACK: *Back*

The person to the right of the person who picked the card drinks. This is because "back" and "jack" rhyme. Is this sufficiently idiotic for you yet?

QUEEN: *Questions*

The person who picked the card asks someone a question and that person must respond by asking another person in the circle a question. If you respond with an actual answer or ask a question back to the person who just asked you, you drink. It would go something like this:

CARD PICKER: (*To person across from them.*) What time is it?

PERSON: (*To you.*) Who is your favorite singer/songwriter?

YOU: John Fogerty.

EVERYONE: Drink!

Are you sufficiently embarrassed to stop playing yet?

KING: *Nothing*

Except that the person who picks the fourth king has to drink the entire beer in the center. Pray this isn't you.

ACE: *Make a Rule*

An example of a rule is that no one may say the word "drink," but can instead say something else that means "drink," like "imbibe!" Ivy League graduates love screaming "Imbibe!" because it sounds fancy. As people get progressively drunker, inevitably a situation like the following will arise when someone breaks a rule:

PERSON WHO CATCHES SOMEONE BREAKING A RULE:
Drink!!

PERSON WHO CATCHES OTHER PERSON SAYING "DRINK":
Ha! Drink!

PERSON WHO CATCHES OTHER PERSON WHO CAUGHT OTHER PERSON SAYING "DRINK": Drink!!!

(*Crowd roars, someone vomits/makes out.*)

Now, I realize that the rules to Kings vary, so, if you happen to be a child who is reading this and says, "No! Five is a chugging contest, not a waterfall!," I say, shut up, loser. This is how I play. Deal with it. If you want to tell your parents how to play a drinking game, be my guest.

RELIGION

Your child believes in God.

~ Or ~

Your child doesn't believe in God.

~ Or ~

Your child doesn't know what they believe.

STAY OUT OF IT.

HOLIDAYS
Eww

Every Christmas Eve my family has a tradition of reading "The Night Before Christmas." This had become an especially awkward tradition, as my grandfather insists that my brother and I wear nightcaps and sit on his lap, though we are both pushing six feet, not to mention twenty-five and twenty-eight, respectively.

— "Sasa"

No matter what your religious affiliation, the holidays are an incredibly difficult time. You may not know this, but your child begins to anxiously anticipate every holiday four weeks in advance, as the memories of the last holiday of its kind begin to surface after being carefully buried for almost a year. The memory of them fleeing, shaken and pale, from the family home as you stood obliviously smiling and waving goodbye is still seared brightly into their memory. For example, it would appear that I have happy childhood memories of the holidays, as the adorable picture of me in a pink onesie bounding down the stairs with a huge smile on my face on Christmas morning would suggest. Yes, this picture is cute, because in it I am five years old. However, my parents insisted on re-creating this pose every year, down to the last detail. I do not want to know where they found adult pink onesies, and I do not want to think about how I believe I saw my grandmother in a similar-looking one the night before, nor that said onesie smelled like mothballs. Guess what my grandmother smells like? In order to drive the point home of inappropriate holiday onesies wearing, I created a flipbook of these pictures, starting at age five and ending at age twenty-five. Flipping through, my parents noticed the dramatic fall of my child's face, and perhaps noticed an extra brightness in my eyes toward the middle of the flipbook. I pointed out that I was subtly giving the camera the finger beginning at age fifteen. The onesie tradition has ceased.

To truly understand the holidays, you must get past the small things. Never mind that this year Granny is slowly losing her mind and is telling the story of how back in her day she called skunks "wood pussies," for the fortieth time in two days. (It was actually funny the first thirty times, but now it's annoying.) Never mind that Grandpa peed on the couch where your child *just sat down*, but they are too polite to get up, and immediately set the couch on fire, mostly because Grandpa is giving them the death stare and is an ex-Marine, and though he's feeble and clearly incontinent, your child still suspects he could do them bodily harm. Forget all of that. Well, I guess you couldn't forget that, because you didn't notice, and herein lies the crux of the holidays: You are so happy that the entire family is together that you gloss over the main problem, namely, that the entire family is together. I'm not suggesting that you don't love your family or that your family doesn't love you. I am saying that any time exceeding three hours spent in the family home with the people who are the exclusive cause of all of your child's neuroses is very stressful. You don't believe that you are the cause of all of your child's neuroses? Remember the time when they sent you a card that on the outside said, "You are the cause of all my neuroses," and on the inside said, "I'm not joking, you really are." You realize that it wasn't one of those hilarious Hallmark cards—it was handmade. It even had sparkles around the words "not" and "really."

Anyway, the worst part about the holidays is that, much like birthdays, they come with the built-in expectation that they have to be a happy and joyous time, no matter how you are feeling in other parts of your life, and no matter how you are feeling toward your family at the time. In fact, do you know that some people have dubbed Christmas "The Most Wonderful Time of the Year"? It's true, and they said it totally sincerely, not even super-ironically while rolling their eyes and making a jerk-off hand gesture. Yes, I realize that the irony of the holidays being far from the most wonderful time of the year has been spoofed many times, most notably in 1989's *National Lampoon's Christmas Vacation*, starring Chevy Chase, Beverly D'Angelo, and a kid who looks kind of like a young Anthony Michael Hall, the third in a wonderful series of films showcasing and commenting on—through comedy and the brilliant slapstick antics of Chevy Chase—the modern American family road trip, European vacation, and Christmas. The 1997 debacle *Vegas Vacation* does not count. Let us never speak of it again.

The buildup of an event as being the best time of the year can only lead to disappointment: If it is not the best time you've ever had, you have somehow failed. If there is anything less than a pristine white Christmas with light flakes of snow falling precisely at the moment your child opens a suspiciously wobbling package and—surprise!—an adorable puppy pops out with a huge diamond engagement ring around its collar as their fiancé emerges from behind the Christmas tree and asks them for their hand in marriage in front of the weeping family and then gives the father a manly shake and you all have a delicious turkey dinner, then you have not had a perfect holiday and you should be vastly disappointed. You also do not live in 1912, which is when the last documented case of that happening took place, so you should be grateful that you don't have to live through two world wars and are going to avoid the pandemic of 1918 as well as the Great Depression.

When you inevitably fail at having the best holiday ever, you will blame the people that were involved in making it less than perfect. This means blaming your family, however deserved or undeserved this blame might be. Maybe your child resents you because they thought that you were giving them the family car (not even a new one, just a 1992 Volvo sedan) so that they could drive cross-country and start their new job, and you didn't. This was especially disappointing, as you kept dropping hints to them like, "You are going to have the *keys* to success," and "This will give you the *drive* to do well in that new job." And then you gave them the old family desktop computer with "No Fear" stickers still stuck to it from when your child put them on there in seventh grade and thought it looked super rad. You pretended to not know why they were upset, having thought that you provided ample clues, in that *keys*=keyboard and *drive*=hard drive. You didn't give them a car on their sixteenth birthday, and they were totally cool with this, even though they always secretly harbored the fantasy of walking out to the driveway and seeing a cool Jeep or something with a huge ribbon tied around it. Where do they get ribbon that big, anyway? It doesn't matter. It just would have made it all the more cool to have a car wrapped in a mysteriously large ribbon, which was probably made especially for them. The ribbon, that is, not the car. Like I said, you did not do this, but instead gave them monogrammed towels, which, though technically made especially for them, do not quite have the same dramatic effect. Plus, there are people in the world who share your child's initials, whereas not many people would have appreciated the presence of a giant ribbon wrapped around a car quite like your child would have. Seriously, why didn't you just give them a goddamn ribbon???

Maybe you don't deserve the blame and you tried to provide your children with the best holiday possible by cooking up great meals and letting them just watch TV when they wanted to and not making them go to excessive amounts of church or family outings. Yeah, right, then you'd be the best parent ever and you wouldn't be reading this book. Instead, you'd be writing the inevitable counterbook, titled, *You Can Stop Being a Fuckup Now*, aimed at kids who have been given nothing but opportunities and support and still can't stop complaining and fucking up their lives. However, I know of no such child like this, so I don't know how well that book would do.

SOME TIPS FOR GETTING THROUGH THE HOLIDAYS

1. EGGNOG. Always have a steady supply of eggnog. Nog is a happy-making drink, until you overdose on it. But certainly you guys know how to be temperate in the face of nog.

2. MOOD LIGHTING. Keep the lights dimmed. Shadowy lighting soothes the nerves and has a calming influence over the entire proceedings. It also allows for hiding in corners if you want to avoid a family member.

3. DANCE PARTY. If you feel the need to start screaming and yelling, simply have an aggressive dance party to let out your frustrations. High kicks and attempted double axels are a must. By the end, you'll be so exhausted and so high off the endorphins, you'll forget what you were fighting about. I suggest dancing to "What a Feeling" by Irene Cara or "Holding Out for a Hero" by Bonnie Tyler.

4. TALKING TRASH. Not to each other! When things begin to get heated, pick on someone outside the family. You could talk about how crazy the foreign-exchange student was that lived with you when your child was in high school, or maybe your wacky neighbor up the street, or even the United States government. When you can all channel your negative energy toward someone else, you become a team. And there is no "I hate my family" in team.

5. BALDERDASH. Have you ever played this board game? It's a board game that simply provides cards with the definitions of strange words that no one knows and everyone writes down what they think the definition of that word is. One person reads all of the definitions, and everyone has to guess which they think is the right one. Sound boring? It's not. For example, let's say the word is "acersecomic." The actual definition is "One who has never had a haircut." However, you don't know this, so you could write down, "A comedian who is not funny." And your child would write, "I wish I were anywhere but here right now." And then you'd read all of the definitions aloud and guess! You know what? Don't play Balderdash.

APPROPRIATE HOLIDAY GIFTS FOR YOUR TWENTYSOMETHING CHILD

1. A subscription to a magazine that will look impressive sitting on their coffee table. (Does not necessarily have to be of interest to your child, and perhaps they don't have a coffee table yet, so it must also look impressive on their floor.)

2. Several volumes of intelligent-looking books, which, when opened, are hollowed out in order to store coins, jewelry, daggers, etc.

3. Chinchilla boots with alligator soles.

4. Pipe tobacco, to go with their new ivory pipe, which matches perfectly with their new cashmere smoking jacket, which looks excellent when they're leaning against their new fireplace mantle in their custom-built country home.

5. Any of the items mentioned in the song "Santa Baby" as sung by Eartha Kitt, including a sable, a light-blue '54 convertible, a yacht, the deed to a platinum mine, a duplex, some decorations bought at Tiffany's, a ring (and she doesn't mean on the phone).

JESUS IN HIS TWENTIES
The Lost Years, Revealed!

Jesus Christ's childhood, adolescence, and early adulthood are famously mysterious. All we know of Jesus is that his birth was a big deal, and then he did awesome things in his thirties, but what of his twenties, clearly the most important time of his life, the period that would shape his miracle-performing years? What was his relationship like with his parents and how did that sculpt his subsequent raising-of-the-dead years? Well, I've managed to compose a rough outline of Jesus in his twenties through modern guesswork and a vague memory of *The Passion of the Christ* and *The Da Vinci Code*. This seems to be the only path he could have led that makes enough sense. What I hope you see from my excellent detective work is that your child is doing exactly what Jesus was doing in his twenties, namely, being a fuckup.

AGE 20: Jesus lives at home in his parents' basement, where he dabbles in carpentry and frankincense smoking. In a myrrh-induced moment of inspiration, he invents and builds the modern sit-down table with chairs. He throws a dinner party and is slightly confused when he turns water into wine simply by wishing it, but doesn't pay too much attention.

AGE 21: Has first sexual experience with the girl next door, whom he has harbored an unrequited crush on for years. He pretends like this isn't the first time he's had sex, because of how embarrassing it is to be a virgin at twenty-one. He confides this to his mother, who relates her own stories of being a virgin and how difficult that was. Jesus gets grossed out and is like, "Mom, for once could you not talk about being a virgin!" Again, he doesn't really question *why* his mother was a virgin at his birth. He just doesn't want to talk about parental sex, or lack thereof, with his mother.

AGE 22: Jesus decides it's time to move out of the house, but he has nowhere to go, so he starts a band with his friends Peter and Paul, and they travel around from town to town, crashing on friends' couches. They are a combination sound of bluegrass and classic rock, but most find them to be derivative. The band eventually breaks up over a dispute about their name: Jesus insists on calling the band "Jesus and the Disciples," but Peter and Paul want to call it "The JPP Experience." They agree with the critics that they suck anyway, and they break up amicably. Jesus will eventually work with Peter and Paul again.

AGE 23: Jesus finally gets a job at the local carpentry store and lives in the back room. His parents supplement his income, because, c'mon, who can honestly live on that salary? He dreams of one day owning his own store and marrying the girl next door who took his V card, but then he hears that she is engaged to another man. This sends Jesus into a deep depression, and he throws himself into his work, determined to win her back.

AGE 24: Jesus is now the most famous carpenter in all the land and has his own chain store and a big house on the Sea of Galilee. One night, he throws a party for all of his friends and his neighbor shows up. She is no longer engaged, and she confesses her love for him. However, he has moved on and is now boning celebrities. In a mustard-seed-snorting-induced haze, he laughs in her face. She leaves, crying and alone.

AGE 25: Jesus becomes engaged to one of his groupies and at a big party at his place on New Year's Eve he walks in on her and his best friend, Judas, doing it in his bed. He demands his ring back, vows never to speak to Judas again, renounces his materialistic lifestyle, and goes to live in the desert, alone.

AGE 26: The Desert Year, as it is more commonly known. Jesus grows an eight-foot-long beard and composes some really crazy music on a reed flute. He doesn't speak for five months, but then he makes friends with a desert rat. The rat tells him that he must return to his life in town, that greater things are in store for him, and that not all women are heartless bitches who steal your soul. He thanks the desert rat and plays a special song that he composed for him on his reed flute. They say farewell, through many tears and heartfelt hugs.

AGE 27: Jesus returns to town to find that Judas has told everyone that he is dead and left his house and business to him. Jesus walks in on Judas while he is giving a big speech to potential investors. Judas turns ghostly white and Jesus casts him out of the office. This is the first time people thought that Jesus had risen from the dead, which is why, when it actually happened years later, the common response was "No big deal, he did it back in 27." Judas eventually comes crawling back, seeking Jesus's forgiveness, which Jesus grants him because he's Jesus effing Christ. This will obviously prove to be a mistake, and Jesus will famously utter, upon Judas's second betrayal of him, "Really? Again? C'mon, this is, like, so cliché, Judas."

AGE 28: Jesus has taken his shop back, but now donates all of his proceeds to charity. However, this is not enough, because he realizes what he has been seeking all these years. It is neither fame nor fortune: He needs to know who his real father is. Mary had never really told him, and Joseph would sometimes get drunk when he and Mary were in a fight and say, "Well, it's not like I can ever measure up to Jesus's *real* father!" And Mary would say, "You're goddamn right!"

AGE 29: Mary finally tells Jesus that he is the Son of God. Jesus's mind is totally blown. At first he thinks that he's just super high, but Mary convinces him that this is the case. When he again accidentally turns water into wine just by wishing it and then makes a blind man see, he is convinced. He quickly becomes comfortable with his new powers and makes friends who look up to him for who he is, not for how much money or success he has. However, his heart remains broken, until he meets Mary Magdalene, falls in love, and they have a baby that they name *The Da Vinci Code*.

THE END

BIRTHDAYS
A Time to Give

I have yet to receive the gift of world peace for my birthday.
Thanks, Mom and Dad. I guess you hate world peace.

— "SWW"

As you already know, birthdays become less and less a cause for celebration the older one gets, unless you're one of those people who age gracefully and look forward to their life ahead, blah blah blah. Anyway, despite their seemingly increasingly rapid journey toward death, your child still enjoys receiving presents. Who doesn't? You might be slightly out of touch about what they might enjoy receiving, since your favorite present as a twenty-five-year-old was your very own bicycle basket, so here are the best birthday gifts you could give them, according to their age.

A TABLE OF APPROPRIATE BIRTHDAY PRESENTS FOR YOUR TWENTYSOMETHING CHILD

AGE 20: Pony

AGE 21: All-expenses-paid bar crawl on ponies

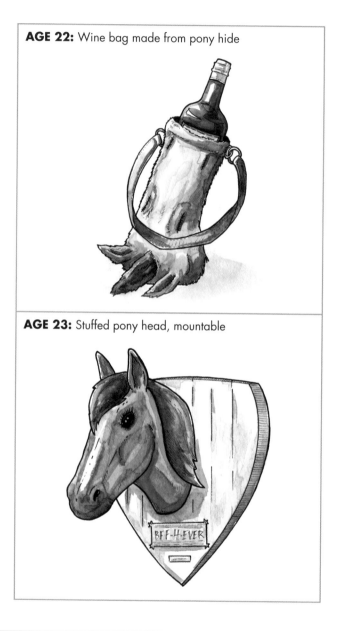

AGE 22: Wine bag made from pony hide

AGE 23: Stuffed pony head, mountable

AGE 24: Preserved heart of a pony in crystal jelly jar

AGE 25: Pony-hair cardigan

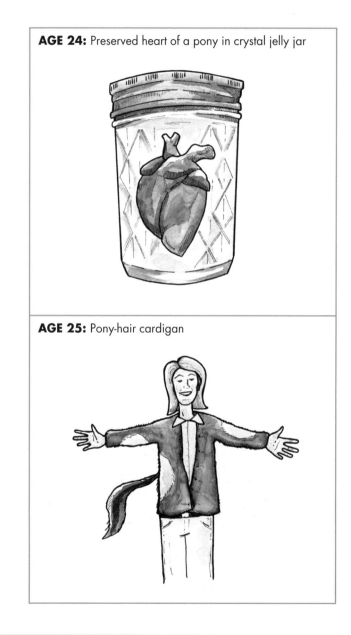

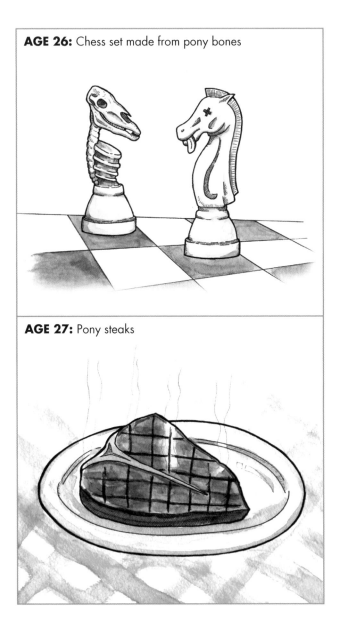

AGE 26: Chess set made from pony bones

AGE 27: Pony steaks

AGE 28: Life-size oil painting of pony

AGE 29: Another pony, as the pony given on twentieth birthday is too old and worn. Old pony goes to the less fortunate.

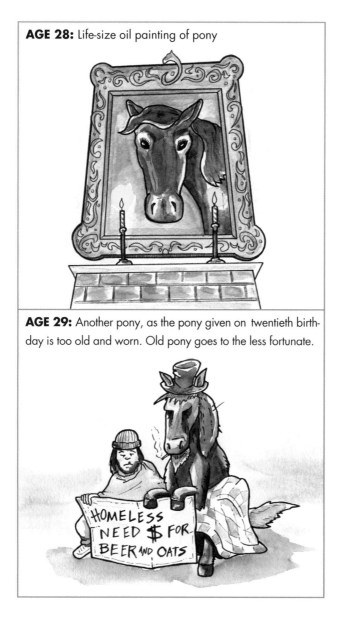

AN ALPHABETICAL LIST OF TYPES OF PONIES YOU COULD PURCHASE FOR YOUR TWENTY-YEAR-OLD

American Walking Pony

British Spotted Pony

Caspian Pony

The Canadian Pony of the Americas

The Chincoteague Pony

Chitty Chitty Bang Bang
(if the beloved flying car were a pony)

Connernara Pony

Dales Pony

Dartmoor Pony

Eriskay Pony

Exmoor Pony

Fell Pony

The Gotland Pony

Highland Pony

Kerry Bog

Lundy Pony

Multiple-Trick Pony

My Little Pony

New Forest Pony

Newfoundland Pony

Nootigedacht Pony

One-Trick Pony

Quarter Pony

Pindos Pony

Pony Express

Pony Keg

Red Pony

Shetland Pony

Show Pony (all types)

Skyros Pony

Tarpan

Unicorn (Unicorns aren't ponies, plus they don't exist.
People use unicorns in jokes too much anyway.)

Welara Pony

Welsh Pony of Cob Type

Welsh Mountain Pony

Zaniskari Pony

A Message from the Author

I have finished all of my raw organic cashews and I'd like some more. Here are some reasons why you should immediately provide me with more nuts.

1. I am still hungry.

2. They are delicious.

3. I did not get paid very much to write this book, and the value of this information to you is priceless, so a little extra gratitude besides the tuppence that you paid for this book would be most appreciated, nay, deserved.

4. I did not name this book *You Can Stop Fucking Me Up Now*, which I had originally planned to do, nor did I name it *Stop With Your Damnable Well-Intentioned Meddling*, which is what my publisher suggested, so you are spared both of those titles, and I deserve proper thanks.

   I'm glad you agree. I shall continue on, strengthened by my fresh supply of raw organic cashews, fuel for the soul.

ROADTRIP!
Probably Less Exciting Than the Film of the Same Name

My dad and I went on a road trip together to my cousin's wedding, driving from Hartford to Virginia Beach. With so many hours together in the car, the subject of his past relationships came up. It was there in the car that I learned that he had been married for six months in 1969 while on an extended acid trip in Morocco, and I may or may not have a half sibling—he wasn't quite sure. He then went on to muse that my current boyfriend looks a lot like his ex-wife.

—*"Srh Wlkr"*

A seminal moment in every young person's life is the drive cross-country, either alone or with a few of their best friends. It represents that final step toward independence and creates a true connection with America and the road. It also tests their ability to make as many references as possible to *On the Road* to whatever member of the opposite sex they are interested in, in an (unsuccessful) attempt to impress them, while deluding themselves that they are half as cool as Jack Kerouac (they aren't[1]). Here for your child is a rough itinerary of

---

[1] More like a millionth as cool as Jack Kerouac! Zing!

a typical cross-country drive, New York to Los Angeles, taking a southerly route:

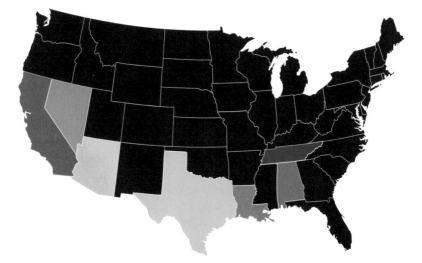

NASHVILLE, TENNESSEE: Your child gets drunk at a dive bar with locals to whom they feel a strong connection, thus debunking the horrible stereotypes that they have thus far harbored about people who live in the South. Having been thusly shamed, they vow to be more open-minded about Southern culture and country music, not just Elvis, even Hank Williams and maybe alt-country, whatever that is. Sounds cool, though.

MOBILE, ALABAMA: They get drunk at a dive bar with locals in an attempt to stick to their vow to not be as condescending about Southern culture. After a close encounter with a tattoo needle and the Confederate flag, your child re-vows to not be as open-minded about

Southern culture. After all, a Confederate-flag tattoo would have seriously taken away from the poignancy of the Chinese-symbol tattoo on their right ankle that means … that means … whatever, it looks rad.

NEW ORLEANS, LOUISIANA: They reflect deeply on the socio-economic divide in America, while getting drunk at a dive bar with locals who seem to tolerate said reflection. Upon consuming late-night jambalaya, your child receives the bowl with the bay leaf. As is the custom with jambalaya, they make a wish, which involves the hot member of the opposite sex at the end of the bar. Their wish does not come true and they stop placing their faith in jambalaya.

AUSTIN, TEXAS: Amazed by the indie-rock scene and hipster culture in Austin, they feel slightly ashamed by all the shit they have talked about Texas. They get drunk at a dive bar with locals, and attempt to start the chant "The stars at night are big and bright …" While waiting for the clapping part, "Deep in the heart of Texas," they get hit in the head with a beer bottle. (But it worked so well in *Pee-wee's Big Adventure!*) Never mind—henceforth, they will talk shit freely about Texas.

GRAND CANYON, ARIZONA: While staring down into the great chasm, they become awed by nature's grand masterpiece, and just feel so connected to life or something, and are convinced that they are more sensitive than their dumb-ass friends (specifically, the smelly, super-annoying ones who they happen to have been driving with in the same car for ten days). They vow to write more, even though it's basically too late for a travel journal, but later they will definitely write more. They'll also look into taking up photography à la Ansel Adams. All of a sudden they have an overpowering desire for weed.

LAS VEGAS, NEVADA: Forget that nature shit. They will speak exclusively in *Swingers* references and will accidentally "double down" because, like an idiot, they were quoting *Swingers* when they should have been concentrating on the game and now have to sleep in the car. They suggest ironically that they should all see Céline Dion and then shamefully realize that they couldn't afford her anyway. However, they do eat delicious eggs, but cannot enjoy them fully, as they are surrounded by morbidly obese people. They begin to feel terrible about everyone in America, particularly everyone in Las Vegas.

LOS ANGELES, CALIFORNIA: Over a delicious breakfast sandwich at the Urth Caffé in Santa Monica, they decide to include avocado in their every meal. They have a drink at the Chateau Marmont, which they decide is the most glorious place on Earth, and they will do everything they can to make it big so that they may live there for three months. Their life's goal has now been made apparent: to live in the Chateau Marmont while they write a screenplay based on their road trip. No one has really experienced America as they have, and their experiences would translate perfectly to the big screen. They will spend the next two weeks thinking exclusively about what actor would play them.

As one can see, you as a parent have no place in this scheme. So, the fact that you are now riding shotgun with your child behind the wheel is truly reprehensible, if not unbelievable. I assume that this is some sort of attempt at bonding. Maybe before you made the leap to a road trip you could've considered a nice phone call first. If you're totally set on the road-trip idea, maybe you could pretend that you're in a limousine together and the reason you can't see each other is because one of you is the limo driver and the other is the passenger and the divider is up between you, so you have to talk on the limo phone. This will also allow both of you to drink alcohol during the phone bonding time, which would be inadvisable if you were driving. Also, you'd save gas and help the environment! Do your bonding with a social conscience.

If you are indeed on a road trip, hopefully you are doing this out of necessity, like maybe you're going to a wedding in St. Louis and have to save your plane-ticket money to pay for hotels and wedding presents. Really, though, if you factor in the gas prices nowadays, plus the cost of staying in hotels along the way to St. Louis, plus meals, are you really saving that much money? What if you get a speeding ticket? That's another two hundo down the drain. And keep your hands off the radio, for God's sake! Yes, traditionally the driver always has authority over the radio, and your child would be happy to listen to NPR with you, especially Terry Gross and *Fresh Air*, but when you adjust the volume of your child's music to an almost inaudible level in a none-too-subtle attempt to get them to change the station, that's just really fucking annoying. Also, playing exclusively Steely Dan and the *Good Morning, Vietnam* soundtrack for eight hours is so not cool. Your child has a wide array of musical tastes and a plethora of knowledge, while you have the track listing to *John Denver's Greatest Hits* memorized. You must trust them with this.

As a result of long periods of time in a confined space together, you will have the opportunity to converse with your child. Your child is aware that there is nowhere to run if the conversation turns sour, unless they have practiced the leaping–from–a–speeding–vehicle–and–rolling–into–a–ditch move they've seen so many times in movies, though they suspect it would probably cause them to sustain a broken limb or three. Therefore, they'll likely rule out that option. Here is a list of conversation topics for you to use on your Child/Parent Road Trip:

CONVERSATION TOPICS FOR CHILD/ PARENT ROAD TRIP
How much you support your child in all of their endeavors
The environment (Isn't it great?)
How old people are scary, specifically Grandpa and his sword collection
National parks in Northwestern America and Canada
French bossa nova
Russian cinema
How you would be happy to do your child's taxes this year
Flowers!
The effectiveness of colonial militias vs. modern-day militias
Miró vs. Picasso

Polar bears: furry friend or dangerous foe?

The English countryside in the 1700s

Stamps

The rise of the American rail system

Croatia as a vacation spot

Weddings (Stop! Just kidding!)

These are literally the only safe topics to talk about. Here is how seemingly innocuous subjects can turn into dangerous fights.

Professional Sporting Events

Segues into talk of high-school basketball career. ➡ You reminisce about how your child broke their nose in a game. ➡ You were never comfortable watching them play after that. ➡ Your child resents that. ➡ **FIGHT.**

Needlepoint

Leads to talk of clichéd phrases that appear in needlepoint, like "Bless This Mess" or "Home Sweet Home." ➡You make half-serious joke about how "Home Sweet Home" needlepoint would have no place in childhood home. ➡What does that mean? ➡ **FIGHT.**

Miniature Portraiture

Leads to talk of noble eighteenth century European families. ➡ Including the Hapsburgs. ➡ You saw the Hapsburg palace during the family trip to Vienna, summer of 2000. ➡ Then you went to dinner, where you ate a lot of Wiener schnitzel, which was gross. ➡ Your child queries why you never took them to an Asian country, where they're sure the food would have been good. ➡ You call them spoiled. ➡ They call you racist. ➡ **FIGHT.**

INTERNATIONAL TRAVEL
Olé!

When I traveled to Spain with my parents, I was the designated translator, as I was the only family member who could speak Spanish. However, my accent being terrible, the Spaniards would insist on speaking to me in their perfect English. This led me to believe that my parents would be able to communicate on their own. So, I left them for one hour and they were kidnapped by gypsies and ended up roaming the plains of Valencia. It was super-annoying getting them back.

— "Sar-ey"

Wow, it is really nice of you to pay for your child to visit London. They would *never* have been able to afford it on their own. In fact, how do people afford to live in London in general? And isn't it crazy how they drive from the wrong side of the car and on the wrong side of the road? If you're a standup comedian, you can use that in a joke, I don't mind. Anyway, like I was saying, I cannot believe that you are paying for their business/first-class plane ticket and a suite at a fancy boutique hotel in Covent Garden! That is so nice! You realize that they want to do their own thing during the day, but perhaps would require some pocket change to get into the Tower of London. You realize that museums are free, but what if they want to buy something? That is far too generous, but, then again, they are your child and they've really been stressing lately about not having a job. Maybe they could find a job in London, or at least a hot Londoner who could maybe put them up in their flat for a couple of months and take them to fancy-dress balls and Indian dinners and such. Going away with your child was really the best thing you have ever done together. And by "together," I mean you spend your entire time there separately, but you are together in bank account.

SEX
I've Said Too Much Already

Once I walked in on my parents having sex, though they didn't see me and continued on. I believe it was standard missionary position, though I can't be certain, as I immediately suffered from hysterical blindness. I ran out of the room, crying, and later ventured back in when I was sure that they were done and sobbed to my mother that I'd had a bad dream. She came into my room and I told her what I had seen and demanded to know why they would be having sex if they already had two children. Was I not good enough? She assured me that since I was twenty-four and she was fifty-five, there was little to no chance that she would have another child. That sort of made me feel better, but that image has stayed with me and these past two weeks have been torture.

— "Sarah"

I am going to write this chapter while peeking out from behind my covered eyes—the prospect of writing about sex, you, and your child is that scary. Consequently, the writing process will be arduous and take at least three times as long as usual, as I will have to type with my elbows. If I'm doing my math correctly, this means that I will write this chapter in about an hour and a half. You see, I am an awesomely fast writer, mostly because I can type very quickly (120 words a minute, it's true) and the advice just flows out of me as though ... as though I were ... some sort of good advice giver. This fact does not necessarily affect your reading process, but I hope that you appreciate what it has taken for me to write this chapter: I have had to TiVo my favorite show, *Dogs With Jobs*. Don't worry about me, I'll see *Dogs With Jobs* at some point, probably in a couple of hours while snacking on some carrots and hummus. I will be left with the heartwarming feeling of seeing a dog with a job, which will help me ease into the recovery process, post-parent-sex-writing ... although then I will sink into a subsequent depression wondering, if a dog can have a job, why are there so many humans without jobs?

In anticipation of writing this chapter, I keep an airsickness bag that I stole from my last flight close by, along with Gatorade and saltine crackers, so that I might press on even after I lose essential electrolytes due to parent-sex-writing-induced vomiting. This chapter is important, yet incredibly unpleasant, much like a root canal or a Pap smear. You see? Ugh, even writing "Pap smear" was gross, just because I know you are reading this right now. Which leads me to sex talk.

You probably had a sex talk with your child when they were about eleven, not because you wanted to, but because your son started screaming uncontrollably at the sight of his giant erection, which he sustained while riding shotgun in the family Volvo on the way to Disney World. Whether it was the heat, the bumpiness of the road, his half-asleep state in which he was thinking about the Little Mermaid, or a combination of all of these factors, you'll both never know. All you know is that stretch of road between Myrtle Beach and Orlando will always be seared in both of your memories as the turning point in your relationship, the moment when there was such a thing as too much information exchanged between parent and child. You have had plenty of those conversations since then. (Let's not forget the Sometimes I Think About What My Life Would Be Like If I Hadn't Married Your Mother Conversation or the I Had My Share of Gay Experiences When I Was Your Age Conversation.) However, as this was the first, it holds a special resonance. As a consequence, your son could only shy away from Cinderella and Belle at Disney World for fear of a repeat incident, and has since beheld Disney cartoon heroines with a mixture of lust and fear. Actually, that's how he views all females. That also marked the first time, though not the last, that you considered Disney World to be a den of sin, which resulted in you registering a formal complaint with Disney World to not have their character actors dress so provocatively. You were, however, mildly relieved that your son was clearly not gay. Not that you would have had a problem with that, you'd love him the same anyway, but at the same time it's sort of nice to know that he would not be visiting Disney World years later with his partner on "Gay Day," because, let's face it, that's just gay.

Perhaps that wasn't the first time you encountered the subject of sex with your child. Perhaps at age five, your child, having awoken from a bad dream, sleepily padded over to you and your spouse's room to seek comfort, only to walk in on you two doing it like nobody's business.

Oh, God. I just got that feeling where your mouth starts to water before you puke. Okay, it's gone.

As your child ran screaming from the room, perhaps you considered pretending like it never happened and denying the entire incident to your child, convincing them that they must still have been dreaming. You wondered if you would have been a different person today if your parents had used that tactic when you walked in on them, and wondered how it was possible that although you made a vow that day to never let your kids see you do it, you had just broken it, and perhaps you could still retain that vow, again, if you convinced everyone involved, including your spouse, that it never happened. However, your conscience got the better of you and you went into their room and assured your weeping child that you were not trying to have more babies because they weren't good enough. Yes, that worked like a charm back then. Your child went to sleep, fears assuaged, peaceful in the knowledge that they were the only child for you … until nine months later when you had their little brother. Good one. And you wonder why your eldest was so tough on your youngest.

However, when you decide to book adjacent rooms with your children at a hotel during a family reunion and think that it would be fun to have loud hotel sex, maybe you should consider that your children can hear everything, they are not eight years old anymore, nay, they are twenty-five, and they (hopefully) understand exactly what you are doing. They cannot help but have a mental image of you two, which is disturbing enough in itself, but then they get to thinking about the fact that they are not having sex and you are, and suddenly you're stuck with a $200 minibar charge the next morning. Really, you deserve it. Yes, good for you that you're super old and are still having sex. Huzzah! But you have to keep that to yourself. Unless you're Pierce Brosnan and Rene Russo in the 1999 remake of *The Thomas Crown Affair* and have inexplicably graphic, albeit hot, older-person sex, all over your twenty-room Upper East Side townhouse, you have to keep your personal affairs under the deepest of covers. Soundproof covers.

As far as talking about sex with your older child, this is strictly off limits. Neither you nor your child should acknowledge that you have had sex, even when your child is about to become a parent. You think this is immature? Okay, maybe you'd rather talk about your favorite sexual position and swap notes with your child. Oh, you wouldn't? But you were so eager to share before, what happened? That's right.

As a corollary, please refrain from any conversations that steer toward grandparent–sex talk. For example, never utter the phrase "I think your grandfather is jealous of my sex life." Nor, when Grandma starts dating someone at the nursing home and your child enquires as to the state of their relationship, should you reply, "Well, it's all about the sex," and then launch into a diatribe about how assisted-living communities are hotbeds of sexually transmitted diseases, however true or untrue this may be. I'm actually surprised that you are so cavalier in talking about your parents' sex life. Maybe it's a generational thing, but what exactly is appetizing at all about (*a*) picturing old people doing it and (*b*) having those old people be none other than your parents?

In order to drive this point home, I will provide you with an excerpt of some of my erotic fiction, which I write on the side under the nom de plume Leslie Haversham. As you read, please picture your parents as the two main characters, Inga and Cormac.

Inga lazily slipped off her negligee and dipped her toe into the steaming hot bath that her manservant, Cormac, had drawn. It was just right. Cormac always drew the perfect bath, an impressive feat for so young and virile a man.

She looked at her naked body in the mirror, admiring her curves. Suddenly, Cormac appeared in the reflection with her.

"Cormac!" she exclaimed. "What are you doing here? I told you to iron my underthings after drawing my bath! How dare you surprise me in such a manner!"

Cormac said not a word, as he locked his eyes with hers in the mirror and slowly enclosed his strong, manly hands around Inga's full, ripe bre—

I'm sorry, I can't do it. Now I'm picturing my parents, and it's just all too much. Here it comes. Where's that bag? I think that little exercise just put me off erotic fiction for a while, which is my main source of income. Great, now I'm going to starve because I'm teaching you a lesson that you should have already known.

Okay, okay, I'm sorry. This is not your fault. You need to know this and no one has ever taught you. I shall continue … but not before you see this drawing of two old people having sex:

Please also refrain from telling your child the story of how they were conceived. Yes, you may have taken the entire family on a really nice vacation to St. Croix, and your children totally appreciate this, especially since they can't afford such luxuries for themselves, but that does not mean that you can recount the story, over a couple of piña coladas, of how twenty-six years ago you and your spouse engaged in crazy tropical-island intercourse that eventually resulted in your child. Furthermore, you need not postulate that the fact that they were conceived in such a hot, tropical clime resulted in their fiery personality. When your child appears to be "hot-blooded" it's probably because they are screaming at you to stop talking about sex already.

In conclusion, please never mention the act of sex, nor utter the word "sex," even in the most sexless of contexts, like "The amoeba has no sex organs" or "Grandma hasn't had sex in forty years"— Oh, wait. Oh, God. Excuse me.

MOVIES THAT YOU MAY NOT WATCH WITH YOUR CHILD BECAUSE OF EMBARRASSING OR GRAPHIC SEX SCENES THAT CREEP UP ON YOU AND YOU MIGHT NOT REALIZE THAT THEY ARE ACTUALLY IN THE MOVIE BECAUSE NO ONE TOLD YOU ABOUT THE SEX SCENES WHEN THEY RECOMMENDED AN OTHERWISE GOOD MOVIE, WHICH YOU SHOULD STILL WATCH, JUST NOT WITH YOUR CHILD

Love and Basketball   (sex-with-neighbor sex)

The Thomas Crown Affair   (graphic middle-age sex)

Heathers (uncomfortable outdoor, though badass, high-school sex)

Prime (Uma-Thurman-with-much-younger-man sex. Several scenes. Uma is seriously charming in this one, so you should see it, but not with your kid.)

A LIST OF ACCEPTABLE MOVIES TO WATCH WITH YOUR CHILD THAT CONTAIN ABSOLUTELY NO SURPRISING SEX SCENES

Bambi

Clue

And that's it.

SOMETHING FOR THE KIDS
Sex in the Parental Home

Hey, kids! Thanks for reading this book. It's really great that you would take the time to read something meant for your parents, unless you're too stoned right now to realize what exactly it is that you're reading. If you're sober, wasn't it impressive how I wrote that sex chapter? Aren't you grateful? You better fucking well better be. Anyway, just as you never want to see, hear, or imagine your parents having coitus, the same goes for you. When you and your significant other come home for a weekend and your parents allow you to sleep in the same room, there are rules that you must follow in order to respect their delicate sense of decorum, cultivated in the fifties, when the sight of a woman's exposed ankle caused fiery demons to rise from the stove at which they were cooking and set ablaze their poodle skirt. Basically, what you should remember is that you should have sex as though you were your parents, growing up in the fifties, which means that their sexual standards when they were at home would be from their parents, which would be like they were living in the thirties. This theory does not extend further back, as sex was invented in 1928 out of necessity when baby-delivering storks became extinct because of lax hunting regulations, and twinkles in eyes were permanently extinguished by more stringent fire codes. Therefore, when sleeping with your significant other in your parents' house, it is as though you should be following the Hays Code, also known as the Motion Picture Production Code of 1930, which was enacted by the Motion Picture Producers and Distributors of America to keep sex out of movies and to uphold morality in film in general. I have reprinted a portion of the Hays Code here, save for the parts that refer to racism and pedophilia, as I trust that you are neither racist nor pedophilic.

Section II of the Hays Code covers sex in film, and states:

The sanctity of the institution of marriage and the home shall be upheld. Pictures shall not imply that low forms of sex relationship are the accepted or common thing.

1. Adultery, sometimes necessary plot material, must not be explicitly treated, or justified, or presented attractively.

2. Scenes of Passion
   a. They should not be introduced when not essential to the plot.
   b. Excessive and lustful kissing, lustful embraces, suggestive postures and gestures, are not to be shown.
   c. In general, passion should be treated so that these scenes do not stimulate the lower and baser element.

3. Seduction or Rape
   a. They should never be more than suggested, and only when essential to the plot, and even then never shown by explicit method.
   b. They are never the proper subject for comedy.

4. Sex perversion or any implication of it is forbidden.

5. White slavery shall not be treated.

6. Sex hygiene and venereal disease are not subjects for motion pictures.

7. Scenes of childbirth, even in silhouette, are never to be presented.

There you have it, all laid out for you. If you were even *thinking* of engaging in white slavery or of introducing scenes of passion when they are not essential to the plot in your parents' house, you can just *forget it*. If you need further reminding of how to conduct yourself, you may tape an FBI warning to the ceiling above your bed, which will remind you that a stiff fee and possible jail time may accompany your breaking of the Hays Code.

PARENTAL VISIT
A Glorious Forty-Eight Hours.
And No More.

My mom came to New York with her boyfriend one weekend when I was out of town and asked to stay in my studio apartment. I said yes and then realized that they would be sleeping together in my bed, possibly even touching. After taking several cold showers to cleanse myself of this mental image, I decided to allow it with the stipulation that they would buy me a new bed once I ritually burned the old one after their stay.

— "S.W."

If you have a highly functional child who has somehow graduated college, found a job, and supports themselves by earning money at said job in order to pay for their life expenses, you are insanely lucky. I really have no idea how you raised someone so competent. Even if your child has a tendency to kick stray dogs or harbors a distaste for happy babies, the fact that they are supporting themselves at such a young age makes them a better person than you or me. Well, mostly you. Look at me, writing a very informative, sure-to-be-best-selling book! Granted, you have probably paid your way through life, starting at age thirteen, when your single mother couldn't provide for all six of you, so you, as the oldest, kept your family afloat by hauling ice up eighteen flights of stairs or you ran off to the big city to pursue your dream of being a famous film actress, only to end up working as a size model for an ornery seamstress who vastly underpaid you. However, as I have mentioned before, advances in time-stopping technology have rendered twenty-eight the new twenty-one, and your child cannot be expected to make the same sacrifices that you did, especially now that even plus-size models are dangerously underweight.

When you visit your financially independent child, a very important rule to note is that though they have done spectacularly and can pay their way throughout the rest of their life, you must treat them as though they have not a dime to their name when you come to visit. No, don't look right through them like you would a homeless person on the street who asks for money and try to placate your guilt by reminding yourself that it is illegal to panhandle and that, moreover, you donate to several charities that help people like this so that you may bypass this uncomfortable personal contact. No, throughout your entire visit, your child must not once reach into their wallet, unless it is to show their old student ID so that you may take advantage of a museum ticket discount. Do not worry, you are not being cheap. Museums are very expensive nowadays. Especially the new MOMA in New York! Twenty dollars a ticket! Can you believe it? I mean, I can look at one in every five computer screen savers and see Van Gogh's *Starry Night* for free!

You are required to provide at least two meals out,[1] preferably dinners, although lunches and brunches are acceptable. Breakfast is, of course, out of the question. Your child is not required to deal with you before 11 A.M., never mind that breakfast is the least expensive meal of the day, unless you get one of those thousand-dollar omelets, but that's just a waste of a grand that you could have given directly to your child as money instead of in omelet form. These meals should take place at restaurants of your child's choosing. They know more about the place where they live than you do, even though you may have lived there for a couple years in the seventies or early eighties, which, although very cool and I'm sure you saw a lot of seminal bands in small venues when nobody else knew about them, was still a long time ago and things have changed. For example, those bands are now old (or dead) and charge too much for shows in amphitheaters (if they're dead, then their cover bands do) and the cute Polish diner on the corner is now an Urban Outfitters.

When visiting, it would also be nice to meet some of your child's friends and take them out for meals as well. By meeting your child's friends, you can easily determine where they stand in the social hierarchy of their inner circle. They will have the funny friend, the token fat friend (possibly overlapping with the funny friend), the smart friend, the hot friend, and the drunk friend.

---

[1]This follows the basic assumption that you will be visiting for no more than two days. Therefore, although a meal a day is the rule (one day in town, one meal required), you may not visit for more than forty-eight hours, hence the two-meal minimum per visit.

Say you take your child and three of their friends out to eat. One of them is portly and gregarious, another is quiet but makes polite and keen observations, and one just gets drunk and familiar too quickly with you, but you can see that they are fun. From this you may conclude that your child is the hot friend. You may rest assured that though they may not be smart or funny, they will probably find love, as they are extremely good-looking. There is a slight chance that your child's friends may not fit into any of these stereotypes, but feel free to mold them in such a way in your mind so that you may more easily form assumptions.

A nice apartment-/housewarming gift is a good idea, something that says, "Thanks for paying your own rent." A check worth a month's rent might be nice. Remember, no matter how much your child is making, whether they are a super-wealthy banker or just getting by as a waiter, money is always welcome. If they are a struggling waiter, they can use it to buy essential items that they might otherwise do without, like fancy Dijon mustards, and if they are a super-wealthy banker, they can use it as rolling papers for their drugs, or simply set it on fire in order to light their cigars. Don't worry, I'm sure they wouldn't use your money for the actual drugs. Remember, if they are considerate enough to pay their own bills, they are considerate enough not to use your cash as drug money. Therefore, cash instead of a check is best in these situations, as a check can only be used once for lighting purposes and doesn't have the same panache as a twenty spot whilst lighting a cigar. Obviously, the corollary to this is that the check may be some sort of symbol of how they don't need your monetary support anymore, in which case it might be a nice gesture for them if they set fire to the check to light a celebratory "I don't need Mom and Dad's money anymore" cigar. They'll specifically request this token check, though, so you can make sure to cancel it immediately.

As far as staying overnight at your child's place of residence, this is strictly forbidden. Even if your child lives alone in a three-bedroom apartment or an eighty-room mansion, it is your duty to spring for a nearby hotel or a bed-and-breakfast for the duration of your stay. If your child lives in a studio apartment, don't even think about it. If your child lives with a roommate, by God, how could you be so crass? It's awkward enough for them to share a living space, let alone a bathroom. Who needs you awkwardly walking out of the shower while the Craigslisted roommate, or, worse, someone you already know, is brushing their teeth? That might prove to be hilarious in terrible situation comedies, but not in the real world.

If your child is out of town and you happen to be in town to see the opera or a musical, do not ask to use your child's apartment. The thought of you and your spouse—or worse, now that you are divorced, you and your significant other—sleeping or doing something unmentionable in your child's bed will prove so loathsome to them that they might cancel their trip altogether. On that trip, they would have met a wealthy entrepreneur who, upon meeting your child, would have decided that they have moxie, and, as eccentric

billionaires are wont to do, they would have immediately made them their protégé and heir to their empire, treating them like the child they never had. If your
child had inherited this empire, you would have never
wanted for money again and would wear very expensive watches attached to chains that you would keep in
your breast pocket. No, money isn't the most important thing in the world, but you would have been extremely happy as well.

If you are in some way contributing to your child's
rent, do not ask them for a spare set of keys. This is
mostly to save you the pain of accidentally walking in
on your child in a very uncomfortable act, a situation
that you should be hypersensitive to, what with the incident of '94. There's no need to go into detail—you remember it, your child remembers it, the family dog has
somehow internalized the event and refuses to be in the
room with you two at the same time. Also, the specter
of you showing up at your child's doorstep out of the
blue will cause them to break into light sweats when
they hear a knock on the door and they will be confronted with your image around every corner, though
when they shake their head and pass their hand over
their eyes you will be gone. They will wonder if it was
actually you, but then suspect that you are following
them. They will eventually have a nervous breakdown,
as they are also coping with the fact that they are haunted daily by the unidentified hook-handed man that they
ran over last summer when they were on a drunken joy
ride with their friends and whose body they threw off
a cliff, after which they vowed to each other never to

speak of the incident again. So, as you can see, they are dealing with a lot right now and the last thing they need is for you to have a spare set of keys.

In the event that your child does let you stay in their apartment, it is your responsibility to treat it with the utmost respect—namely, you may not have sex in their bed. In fact, no touching whatsoever, and you must don head-to-toe flannel pajamas and a Level 3 hazmat suit and immediately wash the sheets upon waking. In the summer months, you may substitute head-to-toe silk pajamas for the flannel version.

Really, your child is excited to see you. The majority of the time, the relationship you have now is one of consenting adults who have entered into a friendship, rather than that of strict parent and petulant child. However, this veneer will quickly melt away, as if by magic, at exactly the forty-eighth hour of your stay, so have your time together, be merry, then go on your separate ways.

MIDDLE-OF-THE-BOOK
SURVEY

Let's check on your progress in this book thus far.

1. Have you accurately and completely grasped the "twenty-eight is the new twenty-one" concept?

2. Would you be able to describe the difference between an Unemployed Creative Child (UCC) and an Unemployed Uncreative Child (UUC) to the child-welfare worker who comes to your house because your child has called them, before they storm off angrily when they realize your child's true age?

3. Can you describe the difference between the geometrical theorems of Side Angle Side (SAS) versus Angle

Side Angle (ASA) or Side Angle Angle (SAA) versus Side Side Side (SSS)?

_____

_____

_____

4. Have you memorized all of the drinking-game rules? Have you then promptly forgotten all of the drinking-game rules, as you have no need for them, right? Right???

_____

_____

_____

5. Do you have the necessary funds to provide your child with a pony/ponies throughout their twenties, including maintenance and housing costs?

_____

_____

_____

6. Are we clear about sex? Don't answer that. Stop thinking about it. Just blink twice if you understand.

_____

_____

_____

SIBLING RIVALRY
One Child Is Probably More Talented Than the Other

My twin sister told everyone during her job-orientation retreat that her twin (me) was mentally retarded. When I met all of them, they were super nice, but I didn't figure out why until later.

—"W., S.W."

In the event that you have more than one child, you are well aware of the causes and effects of sibling rivalry. Basically, and you're not going to say who, but one child is clearly more talented and good-looking than the other/s. If you have twins, this is made especially clear. Isn't it weird how even though they're identical, one twin is clearly better-looking than the other? Ah, Mother Nature! You unforgiving bitch!

Sibling rivalry does not end upon leaving the house. No, quite the contrary—the stakes are only raised in the real world. As a parent, you must do your best to diffuse the sibling rivalry, and I'm sure that you certainly did your best … but sometimes your best is not enough.

When they were young, you encouraged your children to go into vastly separate fields of work so that their lives would not be so directly comparable. Let's say that both your children expressed an interest in the law at an early age. That is, you thought that they said the word "law" when they were probably saying "baw," or some such nonsensical word a two- and three-year-old would say. Excited, you identified the one who held the most potential in the law through a series of rudimentary tests, like placing a gavel before both of them and seeing who banged it in the most convincing manner, or putting them in tiny business suits to see who wore them with the most aplomb. Once the child with the inclination toward the law was identified, you thought it would be best to encourage the other child into a life of crime so that the two would never be competing. Oh, how wrong you were. Cut to twenty years later, when your DA child is hot on the case of his crime-lord brother, only he doesn't know he's his brother because they haven't spoken in fifteen years because the DA brother renounced his criminal brother long ago and the crime-lord brother has changed his name. When they finally come face to face in the bust that your DA child insists on attending, despite the FBI's insistence that they can handle it, they are shocked and appalled. After all, it turns out that it is none other than their very own flesh and blood who they have sworn to their wives and the press and their cohorts to bring to justice/kill. See what you've done? Both are forced to resign from their posts, as they have lost all trust in their respective fields. After all, they were *literally* fraternizing with the enemy.

You might have gone the opposite route, as you realized that sibling rivalry has the potential to take the attention off of you. Perhaps you encouraged both of your children to go into the law and offered incentives, such as trips to Greece and fancy cheeses, to whoever received the best grades and got into the better law school. This crass bribery led to rampant cheating on the part of both of your children, their severe social retardation in America because they only felt at home in Greece, their unhealthy love of cheese, and, of course, an eventual disbarring and hardening of the arteries.

The lesson in all of this is that you have to let sibling rivalry run its course without any interference from you. You may want to physically stop them if they go after each other with fisticuffs, but, other than that, competition is what makes us do better. I wish that my brother were writing a book exactly like this so that mine might be funnier. But he isn't. And you're the ones suffering for it. I'm sorry that my brother is such a failure and in prison. You hear me, John? Write a book so mine doesn't suck! You'll have plenty of time in prison! Mom, Dad, stay out of this.

PRISON PERSPECTIVES WITH JOHN WALKER

Well, Sarah, I'm sorry that I can't find much funny about my *hilarious* sentence of six to eight years in Chino for stealing a golf cart. Yes, I am serving a sentence next to drug dealers and murderers because my drunken antics involved stealing my neighbor's golf cart, which was my third arrest. Seven years ago I was apprehended for stealing a promotional *Star Wars*–prequel cardboard sign, featuring Ewan McGregor as Obi-Wan, from KFC, and four years ago I was busted in the park next to my house for buying a stolen exotic spider monkey. Three months ago, on a dare—from *Sarah*, might I mention—I put on my floor-length Obi-Wan cloak (purchased legally), stole my neighbor's golf cart, and took it on a joy ride around Santa Monica, ending with a crash into a crate of chickens, just like in the movies. Did I also mention that Sarah was riding shotgun and no one arrested her? Mostly because she *ran away*, leaving her only brother to disentangle myself from my robe, which was stuck in the golf cart's axle, which resulted in me standing nude amongst chickens when the police cuffed me. That was my third strike. They hauled me off to jail and now here I am in Chino, the male-only state prison. It's not that it's Sarah's fault. I just blame her. I guess what I'd like to say to all of the parents out there reading this book is that you've done all that you can do. It's just a matter of luck. As in, I am unlucky, whereas Sarah does all kinds of crazy shit and never gets caught. Who could forget the spray-painting-of-school-property-in-full-daylight-in-front-of-a-security-guard incident? They asked her to give the graduation speech after that one. Just pray that your child is lucky like Sarah, and not a police magnet, like me. That, or hope that they lack the scruples to stand by their sibling when things get sticky. That way, they won't be caught. Some say that how you turn out is just a question of nature versus nurture, but I disagree. It's a question of when you'll stop listening to your little sister, who always tells you to do dumb shit, which, when you're in a drunken state, you think is a fantastic idea, or whether you put down the Scotch and say, "Shut up, Sarah. I will do no such thing." I will say that it didn't help that my parents named me after a Scotch. I won't say that it was simply my name that created my addictive personality and predilection for alcohol, but it couldn't have helped. Had I not been named Johnny Walker, I probably wouldn't have been drinking Scotch for five hours before the golf-cart-stealing incident and would be an active member of society today. I guess I'll never know.

FAMILY REUNION
Double the Family,
Double the ... Not Fun

When I went to my family reunion last year, I had a long talk with my cousin who had recently been released from prison. He demonstrated how he'd learned the art of meditation through tai chi, and then caught a moth with his bare hands. Then he ate the moth. Then I left.

— "S. Winston Walker"

About once every five years or so, it is customary to gather the entire extended family together for a long weekend, which sounds great in concept, but has the potential to go horribly awry in practice. The family reunion only happens once every five years for a reason. It's like the Family Olympics. Actually, I guess you could make a pretty good case for *Double Dare*, the Nickelodeon show hosted by Marc Summers, being the Family Olympics. However, timewise, family reunions are like the Olympics in that they happen every five years. Even though the Olympics happen every four years. Look, just forget about the Olympics, okay? The point is, you train for years to get to the point where you can be the best that you can be, so when you see that hot second cousin of yours, even though you would *never* consummate your lust, you can make them seriously rationalize in their heads that making out with a second cousin would be not nearly as bad as making out with a first cousin.

When your children were younger, family reunions were great because they provided your kids with the opportunity to bond with their cousins and meet that second cousin who they would eventually have a totally inappropriate, but nonetheless hot, crush on. It was good, clean family fun. Now that everyone's grown, but not old enough to have kids, and all the cousins are good friends and of drinking age, oh my *God*, do people get wasted. Especially Nana. And that's okay. Yes, I just said that it was okay to get wasted with family. I know that this goes against everything that I've said previously, but—listen carefully—family reunions involve enough people and enough stress that it would be wrong *not* to drink. Unless you're an alcoholic. Then you most definitely should not drink. However, drinking adds to the experience. For example, when your brother's perfect wife is taking a picture with her perfect kids, who are all wearing perfectly matching patterned outfits, you can pretend like you're at one of those interactive *Sound of Music* screenings where you get to drink and yell at the film. You can demand that they all sing "So Long, Farewell." When the children look confused and a bit frightened and your brother gently suggests that you stop drinking, you can get up and start sprinting, pretending that you're running to Switzerland.

If you weren't drunk, you might not think it's amusing when your eighty-four-year-old second cousin twice removed hits on your twenty-four-year-old daughter. With the benefits of alcohol, however, you find him humorously letchy. It sort of reminds you of the time he hit on you when you were twenty-four, except that he was fifty-four at the time, and you can't really decide if fifty-four is creepier than eighty-four. No matter. Either way, it makes you nostalgic to see that your little girl has grown up so fast. Your daughter, however, does not find this incident to be particularly funny or sentimental. But when her second cousin sees her great-uncle hitting on her, maybe he'll get jealous, so she'll deal with it.

What you have to remember as a good parent is that you have no responsibility over your child in these situations. They can field the questions from the dozens of aunts, uncles, second aunts, third uncles twice removed, and great aunts about what they're doing/not doing with their life themselves. This is actually great for you, as you don't have to be the one constantly giving updates about your kids. If someone asks you how they're doing, just point in their general direction, to where they're smoking pot in a field, and go back to sipping your margarita.

DIVORCE
You've Really Outdone Yourself This Time

My parents divorced the year after I graduated from college, which led me to believe that if I were still in school they would be together. So I enrolled in the University of Phoenix online (www.universityofphoenix-online.com). My parents have still not reconciled, and now I have all these goddamn papers to write for my doctorate in Management of Lesser-Known Farm Animals.

— "S. Walker"

Hey, about fifty percent of the married population does it. Divorce is common these days. Now that you've seen one or more children through college and beyond, it's time to take a long hard look at your relationship and realize, thirty years of marriage, shmirty years of … blairriage, you want out. By the way, when telling your spouse that you want a divorce, don't say it like I just said it. The act of divorcing when children are young or even teenaged results in the awkward and frequently bitter sharing of your child, so at least you've spared them that. Instead, you've just crumbled the very foundation of what they would have looked to for help once they realized that, oh shit, they don't know if they're ready to be an adult. However, you have to be true to yourself. Just know that you'll be fucking up your child a bit more than previously expected. Here are some helpful reminders and tips on how to go about the divorce process in a way that will help alleviate the cost of the therapy bill, which your child will naturally and appropriately send directly to you.

PICK AN INSIGNIFICANT CALENDAR DAY TO BREAK THE NEWS OF DIVORCE TO YOUR CHILD, AVOIDING MAJOR RELIGIOUS HOLIDAYS AND BIRTHDAYS.

Notice that this does not include federal holidays. Flag Day or Labor Day would be fine, unless your family puts a near-religious emphasis on the three-day-weekend concept. Also, international holidays are acceptable as well, unless your family has particular ties with Scottish bank holidays. What you should avoid are holidays like Christmas or Passover. For example, if my parents were to tell me that they were getting a divorce on Thanksgiving, I would forever associate turkey, pilgrims, maize, and the Detroit Lions with divorce. This would not be helpful to me, as I'm positive that on some televised celebrity quiz show, which I am sure to appear on at some point in the future after the success of this book, I'll be asked a question referring to the Native Americans' staple crop, and I will be frozen at the buzzer, unable to say maize, as thoughts of my parents' divorce run through my head. I will lose the game, but it's the children's charity I was playing for that will be the real loser.

YOU'RE NOT GAY, YOUR SPOUSE ISN'T GAY, SO DON'T TELL YOUR CHILD THAT ONE OF YOU IS GAY, UNLESS ONE OF YOU IS, AND THAT'S COOL, TOO.

Hurtful things can be flung around in a divorce. Sexuality may be attacked, of course, but these things are said in the heat of the argument, and are meant to disappear into the ether, not to be repeated to your child. If you feel the urge to tell the story where your wife accused you of being gay because you were rehearsing a scene from the all-male production of *The Blue Room*, please do not do so while your child is driving. Driving is a dangerous activity that requires full concentration with both hands on the wheel at all times in the 10-2 position. So, for example, if in the future I have to tell my son that my husband accused me of being a lesbian, instead of saying, "Your father thinks that I'm a lesbian. Well, I think he's gay," I would soften that statement so my child did not immediately swerve the wheel and send us both over Dead Man's Bluff, which I'm sure my future town will have. Or a Blind Man's Chasm. Or a Limping Man's Ravine. Anyway, instead of using the word "lesbian," I would refer to the beautiful Greek island of Lesbos. Instead of using the word "gay," I would say "happy," which means the same thing as some definitions of "gay." Notice how the revised sentence is significantly less traumatic: "Your father thinks that I'm traveling to the beautiful Greek island of Lesbos. Well,

I think he's happy." In my son's subsequent confusion, I will reach over, put my foot on the break, stop the car, take the keys, and tell him what actually happened, saving us from a certain death from plummeting off of Mute Susan's Bridge into Laughing Skeleton Gorge.

IF YOU START DATING YOUR MUCH YOUNGER YOGA INSTRUCTOR, POST-DIVORCE, PLEASE ACKNOWLEDGE THAT THIS IS A CLICHÉ.

Several studies have shown that yoga is healthful to the body and spirit … and apparently to your libido, since it took you all of three months after your divorce to start dating your yoga instructor. Score! However, please do not deny the fact that dating your yoga instructor is the new middle-age postdivorce cliché, akin to running off with your secretary. Again, nothing wrong with this, you just do not have the right to  get defensive when your child rolls their eyes when you tell them about your new significant other. You might also want to consider that your new significant other was your child's yoga instructor, too, and now there is no way that they will go to class, depriving them of this essential healthful exercise. As a result, they run the risk of becoming much less flexible, and are ten times more likely to pull a hamstring while running on the treadmill. Because of this injury, they will not be able to make it to work the next day, which will waste a vacation day that they were planning on using for a long weekend to the Cape with their significant other. This will result in a needless fight and a couple of days of no speaking. Therefore, if you are going to date anyone, consider dating a meat distributor or drug addict, as this will put your child off either red meat or drugs, two things that are very bad for them.

YOUR CHILD DOES NOT BELIEVE THAT THE DIVORCE WAS THEIR FAULT, SO THERE IS NO NEED TO TELL THEM THIS OVER AND OVER AGAIN.

If you keep reassuring your child that the divorce was not their fault, no matter how much they believe this to be true, your repetition of this fact over time will lead them to doubt themselves. This is a form of reverse psychology. The most well-known example of reverse psychology is in Mark Twain's *Tom Sawyer*, when the irrepressible Tom pretends to be *enjoying* his job of whitewashing a fence, and hence draws in his other friends, who not only finish the job for him but pay him to do so. This is an example of successful reverse psychology and excellent writing, akin to this book, which is very, very fun to write. It's so much fun, I don't want to share the job with anyone! There is no way that there is a better job in the worl—huh? Oh, well, I guess you could help me if you have some examples of your parents fucking you up. Oh, you do? Okay, well, I don't know, it's kind of my boo—one hundred dollars, you say? I don't know … five hundred? Well, okay, I guess I could let you write it for just a bit. Here, sit down.

—
— ?
—

You're done? Wow, that didn't take long. That's all you wrote? Well, thanks for the three hyphens, friend. Sorry, yes, and a question mark. No, you can't have your five hundred dollars back. I've already spent it. Yes, in five minutes I spent it. Online. Good day to you, I have to finish my book.

TRUST THAT YOUR CHILD WILL ASK ABOUT YOUR MENTAL HEALTH WHEN THEY CARE TO HEAR ABOUT IT.

You need not reassure them every day that you are "doing fine." If you, in phone conversations, messages, and e-mails, repeat the mantra "I'm doing fine" to your child, it starts to sound like a chant. Some chants, like cheers, are fun. An example of this is "Be aggressive! B-E aggressive! B-E-A-G-G-R-E-S-S-I-V-E!" However, some chants are scary. Perhaps the best example of this is in *Indiana Jones and the Temple of Doom*, when the Indian pagan priest chants "Kal-ee ma!" over and over again, as he rips the still-beating heart out of the chest of the human sacrifice who is strapped into a metal cage, about to be lowered into the pit of fire. You don't want to be the one to pull someone's heart out of their chest. Even if that kind of supernatural power appeals to you, it's still wrong. So stay away from chants.

IF YOU LOSE SOME FRIENDS IN THE PROCESS OF DIVORCE, PLEASE DO NOT TRY TO MAKE UP FOR THIS DEFICIT BY BEFRIENDING YOUR CHILD.

It is a harsh reality that, postdivorce, many of the friends that you shared with your spouse may no longer be your friends. However, in order to compensate for this, do not attempt to befriend your child. Your role as a parent is distinct. For example, if you go to Six Flags together, you shouldn't purchase the picture of you two descending in the water luge together, since that is a purchase only friends may make. However, you may buy them lunch, post-water-luge, as this is something a good parent would do. You could even win them a giant stuffed animal, even though this is bordering on significant-other actions, but it's still a nice gesture, since, really, they didn't want to go to Six Flags in the first place. Then again, neither did you. That's a communication issue you two should work out.

CONSIDER KEEPING YOUR NEW LIVING SITUATION PRIVATE UNTIL YOU FIND LESS-DEPRESSING LODGING.

If immediately postdivorce you are forced to find new lodging, please avoid depressing places like corporate housing or the Days Inn off your local turnpike. This will not only do nothing for your morale, but it will also depress your child to think that you are living on the turnpike where they used to go-cart ironically in high school. If your child is depressed, they will watch a lot of TV and probably take advantage of your Days Inn HBO and Showtime channels. So I guess that means that they'd visit you a lot, which is good for you. However, if you care for your child, you will keep them away from the turnpike Days Inn, as they will take to it too kindly and eventually become night manager there. Then, if you want to bring someone home in an attempt at rebounding, you'll run into your child, now the night manager, and that will just be awkward.

YOU ARE NOT THE FIRST PERSON TO CHANGE THEIR EATING HABITS POSTDIVORCE.

Postdivorce, if you should embrace a healthy lifestyle and diet, do not assume that you are the first to embrace this healthy way of living, as many people have discovered the benefits of, say, vegetarianism, from Gandhi to Alec Baldwin. I just wanted to write that because probably no one has ever mentioned Gandhi and Alec Baldwin in the same sentence. Or Gandhi and Alicia Silverstone. I didn't say Paul McCartney because someone has probably said Gandhi and Paul McCartney in the same sentence before. Anyway, when you take your city-dwelling child to a Japanese restaurant in Middletown, Rhode Island, you may assume that they have eaten sushi before. After all, they do live in

New York City. Therefore, there is no need to explain what miso soup is. Wait, did you just say "misu"? It's pronounced "mee-so." Please do not try to tell them about Japanese food again. They order from the sushi place on the corner all the time. Do you know what hijiki is? Exactly.

This is hijiki.

KEEP YOUR MOTHER AS YOUR MOTHER, AND YOUR BEST FRIEND AS YOUR BEST FRIEND.

In the same way that you should not try to befriend your child during and after the divorce, it is equally as forbidden to become best friends with your mother. Perhaps she has been there for you, but you should really be hanging out with people your own age, even if they do serve wine at dinner at her nursing home on Saturdays. Okay, even if you really love hanging out with your mother, it does sound creepy when you tell people that your mother is your best friend. That information is best kept secret, much like how I keep secret the fact that I can't play the guitar even though I display one in my apartment, and when people ask me to play I dramatically yawn and say that it's high time I went to bed, even though it's noon.

SOME WORDS ON THE UNIVERSITY OF PHOENIX ONLINE

You may have noticed that the person who gave the anecdote at the beginning of the divorce chapter went to the University of Phoenix online and shared my last name and first initial. Well, this may surprise you, but that person is actually … me. I know, I know. I'm sorry about being so coy about my identity, because upon further thought, I think that it's only fair that I take a moment right now to let you know about the exciting opportunities that the University of Phoenix (online) has to offer. Online education allowed me to pursue my dream of running and maintaining my very own farm, and to earn a Ph.D. in the study of Lesser-Known Farm Animals (mice, spiders, etc.). Of course, this farm had to be online, too, as I live in New York City. With my degree, I was able to create my own utopian virtual farm. Although I had to hire a webmaster to create, design, and maintain the actual site, as I know very little about computers, and I did not earn a degree in computers, I was able to instruct the webmaster on the nuances of a farm. As my specialty is in Lesser-Known Farm Animals, some Better-Known Farm Animals (goats, ducks) and

Well-Known Farm Animals (pigs, sheep, cows) are missing, but what my virtual farm lacks in those animals it more than makes up for in the special, unsung, but also very important, farm animals. In one instance, I specified to the webmaster exactly where a spider would weave a web (the upper left-hand corner of the barn doorway). Making the farm as accurate as possible is very important to me. For example, many people without a degree from the University of Phoenix online would assume that spiders frequently weave messages into their webs in order to save well-known farm animals' lives. Well, let me tell you, spiders on farms are not altruistic in that manner, and would screw over their best friend if it meant a payday. All these things and more I learned from my online degree. I am actually grateful for my parents' divorce, as without it I would have never joined the University of Phoenix (the largest accredited online university) and opened so many doors for myself, and for a mere $30,000 you can do the same. If you'd like, you can send me the check for $30,000 and I can give it to the online dean at the University of Phoenix online, as I know him very well. We're meeting for coffee later today, in a Web chat, of course. I'll put in a good word for you. Just send that check and I'll take care of everything. It's never too late to get an education.

DEATH:
Please Don't Make It Suck Even More

My mother thought that it would be appropriate to deliver the news of the death of our beloved family dog, Major, via e-mail. This was very distressing, and made me fearful to check my e-mail, as I couldn't help but anticipate bad news in every unopened e-mail. As a result, I failed to open an e-mail I received from JetBlue Airways and missed out on a great deal to San Francisco, not to mention the friendly banter of the JetBlue staff, which always assuages any fear of flying that I have. Instead, I flew the now defunct Song Airlines, got gouged on the price, and the flight crew made bad jokes,[1] like they were trying too hard to be funny.

— "S.W.W."

Death is a very serious matter, which should be dealt with in a sensitive manner. No matter how old your child is, they will look to you for comfort when they face death. Well, that is, unless you're the one who's

---

[1] On one of my JetBlue flights, the captain got on the intercom and said, "If everyone could just look to their right … Wait for it … We just flew over my house!" I thought this was extremely charming and I laughed heartily. On a Song flight, however, the flight attendant said, "Everyone buckle up, this is the captain's first time flying! Just kidding, folks." I mean, c'mon!

dead, and in that case they'll have to do without you. Forever. Sorry.

Since they are now an adult, you need not try to explain the mysteries of life and death to your child as you once did—for example, as it relates to their pet tadpole, Fluffy (so named out of spite because you wouldn't give them a kitten), or the great-aunt they never knew (also named Fluffy, a nickname acquired later in life for reasons unknown, but you have your suspicions).

Most likely, the responsibility will fall on you to break the news of a family member's death to your child. To be the bearer of bad news is a very difficult task and requires a combination of sensitivity and directness. You don't want to beat around the bush and try to avoid the topic for as long as possible and then realize that you're being ridiculous and then blurt out the news. For example, let's say that you call your child up to deliver the news that their grandmother, your mother, has died. "Hi, sweetie! Well, the yard looks great, I just planted the tulips and put up some white lights in the garden and got out the patio furniture—yourgrandmotherisdead." Yes, you, too, are likely very upset by this news (unless you're not, but we won't go there), but that is no excuse to pair news of patio furniture with the passing of your mother, even though your mother did particularly enjoy that one chaise lounge. Maybe she could have helped with the dishes once in a while if she hadn't loved that chaise lounge so much. You know, why didn't she just ask that chaise lounge to be her daughter? She certainly liked spending more time with it than she did with me—I mean you—I mean—I HATE YOU, MOM! What? I'm sorry. Moving on.

As a corollary, in an attempt to avoid springing the news on them, don't try to find a clever transition to ease them into the news. You don't want the conversation to go like this: "Hi, honey. Well, I just installed the air conditioner in the kitchen, which will be a life-saver, since it's supposed to be really hot this summer. Well, not literally a lifesaver. I doubt it could bring your grandmother back to life! She's dead." Granted, maybe in the future some genius (maybe your unemployed child) will actually invent a device that acts as both a bringing-back-to-life machine (there will be an easier way to say that in the future) and an air conditioner. It would be called the KooLazarus. With a flip of a switch, you would be kept from the cruel summer's heat and watch your mother, your child's grandmother, rise, as if by magic, from the dead.

As this will be the future, the sight of a dead person coming back to life won't be as scary as it would be if you saw it now. If you saw that now you'd probably take a shotgun to your rising-from-the-dead mother thinking that she was a vampire or zombie or something and part of the first wave of a vampire/zombie invasion.

No, in the future, what with the incredible success and prevalence of the KooLazarus, the sight of the dead rising again will be no big deal. I mean, you won't be completely jaded to it ever—how could you be?—but you won't freak out completely like you would if you saw it happen now, having no knowledge of the

KooLazarus. Anyway, you'll turn it on and you will sit back as the cool air blows on your face and enjoy the sight of your mother opening her eyes, sitting up as from a nap, asking for a glass of lemonade, and remarking on the nice, refreshing room temperature. Then she'd probably start telling you to sit up straight and recounting boring stories that you've heard a million times about her childhood in Texas and you'd wish that you never dropped ten grand on the damn KooLazarus.

THE VERY WORST WAYS TO CONVEY NEWS OF DEATH

Voicemail of Death

The very worst thing you could do when delivering the news of death to your child, which may not even cross your mind, as it is too ridiculous, but you never know how you'll act in a traumatic situation, is to leave a voice message of death. Picture it: Your child wakes up from a night out on the town. They have three messages. Groggily they check them. The first one, sent at 4:12 A.M. is from their inebriated friend Rusty: "OHMYGOD, dude, you have to come here—we're all WAAAAAAS-TED!!!!" Second one, sent at 5:37 A.M., from an even more inebriated Rusty: "WHERE ARE YOU? WE'RE DOING KEG STANDS! IT'S SO COLLEGE!!!! (*Barfing sounds.*)" Third one, sent at 9:12 A.M.: "Son, it's your father. Your grandfather is dead." Buzz kill! Plus, is Rusty okay? He sounded pretty sick in that last message. Seriously, a voice message is no place for dire news.

If you are to leave a Voicemail of Death, do so in an efficient manner. Never ramble on in a voicemail about death so that the machine cuts you off. For example: "Son, it's your father. Your grandfather passed away last night. So … if you want to call me, you should probably do that. Or don't. Or wait a while and collect yourself and then call. Actually, you should probably call right now so we can talk about the funeral. You'll probably be staying at Grandma's neighbors' house, since everyone else will be staying at the actual house. It's a nice house. They're from Turkey—the neighbors, that is—so I think that you should find the décor interesting. I mean, I don't know if you're interested in Turkish culture, but it's sort of like Cuban culture a little, or so I've heard, and I know you like Latin stuff, like that Shakira girl, but, point being, your grandfather is dea— (*Beeeeeep.*)" In addition to the excessive rambling, it is not appropriate to ever mention Shakira and your child's grandfather in the same sentence, as the feelings that your male child has for these two people separately could become dangerously intertwined, causing confusion, sweating, and even gayness.

Consequences of a Voicemail of Death

If it is your practice to leave Voicemails of Death, your child might conclude that it is okay to deliver other types of important news via voicemail. They might infer that it is perfectly acceptable to break up with their fiancée over voicemail and consider it a done deal and will forever be known as that dick who broke up with their fiancée on voicemail in some sort of allusion to a bad

Sex and the City episode. Well, I guess in that one where Berger broke up with Carrie via a Post-it note, but you get the point. God forbid they start employing bad puns to explain away their promiscuous and ultimately empty lifestyle. Whatever. I don't care if you liked the show and the sassy female leads and you have all the seasons on DVD. I'm trying to tell it like it is here.

Text Message of Death

It should go without saying that text-messaging about death is off-limits. Text-messaging is inherently a mind-fuck anyway. Your child has probably spent hours poring over one text message from a significant other wondering if it means exactly what they think it means or if they wrote it sarcastically or if it was a reference that they didn't get, and why haven't they responded yet to the text they wrote back? Was it sent wrong? And, for the love of God, why don't people just pick up the phone anymore?? Point being, though there is no nuance to be had in it, it is a double mind-fuck to check a text and find that it says, "Grndpa=Dead." Actually, your child is probably such an expert at interpreting text messages that they might overinterpret it and think that their grandfather is merely metaphorically dead to you. Thinking it was a joke, they'll laugh about it to themselves and then sit bolt upright in the middle of the night, suddenly realizing that their grandfather is indeed dead.

Consequences of Text Messages of Death

Misinterpreted Text Messages of Death will lead your child to question their text-message-reading abilities, of which they had previously been very proud. It will cause them to agonize over every incoming text from that point on, wondering if there is a hidden message of death imbedded in each one. For example, if a friend they are supposed to meet up with texts them, "Getting off the subway now," your child, now text-death paranoid, will assume that their friend means "the subway of life," or that their friend accidently typed "off" when they meant "under." They will be worried for their friend's well-being until they finally see each other and your child clutches their friend in a sobbing embrace. The friend will be freaked out and probably not want to hang out with your child that much after that, no matter how good their weed is. Did I say weed? Your child doesn't smoke weed, I don't know why I said that. I mean, weed smokers wouldn't be paranoid and overemotional at all. That's ridiculous. Your child is probably an eccentric poet or something. A real Emily Dickinson type.

E-mail of Death

In one case study a woman checked her e-mail and found a message from her mother informing her that the beloved family dog had died at the age of fifteen, which is an old age, something like five hundred years old in human years, give or take. No one has yet found a set number that is the equivalent in dog years to one human year.[2] The fact that the mother did not even bother to pick up the phone to relay this news

---

[2] In addition to solving global warming and earthquakes, an unemployed child could probably figure out the equivalent in dog years to one human year. Wait, I'm being told that it's seven dog years to one human year. Oh.

merely added to the distress felt by the daughter and she spent all night wondering how her mother could throw the dog a birthday celebration every year, complete with a birthday cake—which the dog technically could not partake of, what with chocolate being poisonous to dogs—yet feel the need to convey his passing electronically.

Consequences of E-mail of Death

Now the daughter is afraid to check her e-mail and missed out on potential great deals from JetBlue Airways and paid way too much for her plane ticket to San Francisco, because instead of responsibly checking her e-mail, where she would have read a message describing the great rates on JetBlue, she went to Expedia.com, because she had been watching TV instead of keeping up with her e-correspondence and she liked how in the commercial they sang "dot com!" She also associates birthday cakes, once her favorite genre of cake, with dead dogs, and now prefers erotic cakes, which is actually her own problem and has nothing to do with the association with the dead dog, or at least let's hope not. At some point, you may want to snoop around your child's room if they are living at home or go to their apartment and see if they are stashing any erotic cakes in their sock drawer. Indulging in erotic cakes is a deviant practice, not to mention bad for the waistline, and could ruin many a sock. Families have been torn apart by a single individual's addiction to erotic cakes. If you find any, you should immediately set up an intervention. Please call 1–800–

END-CAKE for a free and anonymous support line. It's never too late.

Clowns of Death

Perhaps you think that since death is so depressing, you must counteract the bad news with levity, like by hiring a clown. You may not be aware of this, but there are countless references to how scary clowns are, and it has been scientifically proven that 89.5 percent of people suffer from fear of clowns, or coulrophobia, and 60 percent of these people think they're the only one who's afraid of clowns and like to mention it sometimes at parties like it's some sort of interesting and humorous fact about them. These people are annoying. It should go without saying that your child associates clowns with the 1990 made-for-television movie *It*, as adapted from master of horror Stephen King's novel of the same title. In *It*, the psycho serial murderer is a clown, as played by the excellent Tim Curry, and almost everyone has stayed home sick and watched the TBS midafternoon presentation of *It*, which, I have to say, is a poor scheduling choice on TBS's part, what with the plethora of sick children who watch midafternoon TV after the presentation of *The Price Is Right* at eleven.

Consequences of Clowns of Death

As a result of receiving a Clown of Death, your child will actually have reason to tell people at parties that they are deathly afraid of clowns. However, since they have done this before with abandon and people now suspect that they aren't actually afraid of clowns—

because who talks so cavalierly about a serious fear?—a boy-who-cried-wolf scenario will ensue and the next time they are confronted in a dark alley by a murderous clown and scream with terror, no one will run to their aid because everyone will think, "Oh, Rob is just pretending to be afraid of clowns again. Let's go grab a Fresca." Even if your child's name is not Rob, they'll call them that because they don't care to remember the name of someone who won't stop talking about clowns all the time. They will grab a Fresca, though, as they are delicious.

Singing Telegram of Death

I know what you're thinking. "If I can't hire a clown to convey the news of death, I'll order a singing telegram." Well, you are wrong. Dead wrong. Although this is a lesser-known phobia, your child does associate singing telegrams with the 1985 movie *Clue*, in which a young woman is shot in an unceremonious manner while singing a telegram. (Spoiler: It was Mr. Green, as played by Christopher Lloyd, who shot the singing-telegram girl, whom he had had an affair with when she was his patient, as she was a potential informant to his blackmailer, Mr. Boddy, as played by the once again excellent Tim Curry.[3])

---

[3] It is no coincidence that Tim Curry has been mentioned twice in connection to your child's phobias, but this is not to disparage this actor's actor; rather, it is to highlight his incredible chameleon-like ability to completely morph into his characters and leave an indelible impression on the hearts and minds of your children. I recommend going to the Internet Movie Database (www.imdb.com) to see for yourself what an amazing oeuvre Mr. Curry has built up over the years.

Consequences of Singing Telegrams of Death

There are no real consequences of a Singing Telegram of Death, although you are employing someone who has committed their life to an obsolete form of communication in song form. You shouldn't encourage them. In fact, you should recommend that they attend the University of Phoenix online and get a degree in a real career, like I did. Again, you may direct them to me and I will help them get started with the check-writing process and whatnot.

COMPARISONS AND COMPETITION
Your Child's Great As They Are— Unless They Aren't

My father told me that he'd pay me $300 to compete against him in the annual Thanksgiving-morning 5K in my hometown. He had been training for months and wanted to prove that he could still beat me. I said okay and took the $300, then pretended to sprain my ankle one mile in, just so he could feel good about himself.

— "Sarah Winston Walker"

You probably already know that while they are growing up it's unhealthy to compare your children to siblings, cousins, neighbors, friends, or scarily precocious child actors. For example: "Congratulations for coming in second in the high jump at your class Field Day! Did you know that Anna Paquin just won an Oscar for her role in *The Piano* and she's your age?"

This does nothing to help your child's personal growth, and rather than stir up a competitive spirit, it will likely make them anxious, and, later, resentful that you did not appreciate them for who they were, and, much later, morbidly pleased and subsequently ashamed when the formerly precocious child star turns into a drug-addled failure. This has not yet happened, and probably will not happen, to Anna Paquin, as her career seems to be going quite well. Not that I care.

Of course, you probably made such comparisons privately, wondering why your brother's son Kenneth, who is the same age as your child, managed to captain his high-school soccer team, play first cello in the orchestra, serve as president of the student council, and get into Princeton as an early-decision admission, while your child was cut from JV soccer his senior year and referred to the school orchestra as the "dorkestra," which, although funny and true, did not help his résumé. In fact, you went a little overboard with the comparisons, drawing up elaborate charts directly comparing each aspect of your child's life to Kenneth's life, and experienced an awkward moment when your child stumbled upon them. You hastily explained to them that the charts were actually part of a new family game show that you were creating, which had to remain top secret, and that you couldn't even mention it again, just to ensure that no one stole the idea. Fortunately, your child, being not very precocious, was satisfied with this answer. If your child had been Kenneth, or Anna Paquin, you would have had a lot more explaining to do.

That was fucked up then, but it's never too late to take steps to stop fucking up your child. I know you can do it—look at your child now! Now that they're out of college, they have actually turned out to be a nice, normal, well-adjusted person, whereas Kenneth is now addicted to porn and his old-school Sega gaming system. I bet your charts didn't see that coming! So you can relax. However, a subtle change has occurred.

Instead of comparing your child to their insanely accomplished cousin, you are now comparing them to yourself. The upside of this is that you consider them to be an adult, which is great, except that you fail to see that your competition with your child is annoying and embarrassing for all those who witness it, including your child. For example, do not try to prove how young and fit you are by insisting that you and your child run a 10K on Christmas morning in 10-below weather. What does this prove? That even on Christmas deadly frostbite exists? I'll tell you this much: In 90 percent of the athletic competition that you try to engage in with your child when they are in their twenties and you are God knows how old (but surely really old), they will best you. Not even by a little—they will outright crush you. Remember when you were a small child and you picked on an even smaller child by putting your hand on their head and telling them to try to hit you and they would just swing and swing and never touch you and they'd be all like, "Gee whiz, what's the big idea?" That's what it'll be like, only you're the one that'll be flailing your arms and saying "Gee whiz," and your child will be so taken aback by this old-timey speak that they'll abruptly drop their hand and you'll fall crashing on your face.

If you consider chess or backgammon to be a sport, maybe that would fall into the 10 percent of victories that you might achieve. But it's not worth it for you or your child to suffer from the first- and secondhand embarrassment that comes along with athletic competition between the two of you.

If you have already realized that your body is no match for your child's young, attractive one in physical activity, maybe you will resort to a more insidious comparison—namely, your weight. When someone who is much older says, "I'm the same weight that I was in high school," there is no one who is impressed by this or happy for them. In fact, that is one of the most annoying sentences ever uttered, only surpassed by "You look tired." Or "You remind me of a late-career Beverly D'Angelo." However, while the proper response to these latter two remarks is "What the fuck is that supposed to mean?" the correct reply to the weight remark is "Shut the fuck up." Notice that when someone says you look tired, or like Beverly D'Angelo, although it is recognized as an annoying statement, it also creates insecurity on the part of the receiver, and the utterer of the execrable declaration, although an asshole, has the power. However, when someone states that they are the same weight as they were in high school, that person is merely an anorexic braggart and a possible liar. They have nothing to gain by uttering such an insipid phrase, except maybe to imply that the person on the receiving end of this statement is overweight because they are not the same weight as they were in high school. However, this is so idiotic that it is not even to be considered. Either way, you must now see why saying something like that to your child would be very fucked up. What did you say? You're not the same weight that you were in high school? Oh. Fatty.

In order to further expose myself to you to gain your unerring trust, here is the chart my parents used to compare me to my cousin of the same age, Laura, at age twenty-three, which I discovered last year, when I found it taped to the bathroom mirror in my old room when I was home for Christmas. My mother must have assumed that I wouldn't look in the mirror because I am so confident in my good looks. Otherwise, I'm sure she would have hidden it more artfully.

SARAH	
JOB	Writer (none)
INCOME	$10,000/year
LOOKS	Wears hair in bun too much
BOYFRIEND	None (gay?)
APARTMENT	Basement studio, cockroaches, sightings of other vermin
ATHLETICISM	Very skilled at basketball and soccer (gay?)

COMMON SENSE	Fair, but no boyfriend (gay?)
ARTISTIC ABILITY	Creates rage-filled paintings on driftwood
LITERACY	High, as a writer, but might benefit from a self-help book
MATHEMATICS	Can tip 20 percent if she uses a tip cheat card
SENSE OF DIRECTION	Excellent, though too prideful in her knowledge of New York City geography. It's a grid, get over it.
AMBITION	Apparently none, except to drink cheap wine and develop crushes on bartenders. She also wants to lose ten pounds.
SOCIAL SKILLS	Drinks a lot
RELIGIOUS BELIEFS	Renounced the church around Chart #18, breaking mother's heart

LAURA	
JOB	Investment banker
INCOME	$200,000/year
LOOKS	Natural blonde(!)
BOYFRIEND	Live-in boyfriend of two years, also investment banker
APARTMENT	One-bedroom loft, Tribeca
ATHLETICISM	Pilates and yoga
COMMON SENSE	Excellent (boyfriend, not gay)

ARTISTIC ABILITY	Glazes ceramic mugs for friends' birthdays, making delightful gifts
LITERACY	Writes a fantastic thank-you note
MATHEMATICS	Deals with complicated numbers every day with grace and aplomb
SENSE OF DIRECTION	Has her driver take her everywhere
AMBITION	Would love to keep her family in comfort for the rest of their lives by giving something back by working hard
SOCIAL SKILLS	Witty conversationalist
RELIGIOUS BELIEFS	Devoted Episcopalian, volunteers at her church's soup kitchen

Okay, let me just say that Laura is a condescending bitch, and not completely real and down-to-earth like me. Just because she happened to excel in math and economics and my talents are of a more wordsmithyish bent does not mean that I have to be punished for not making as much money as she! (As her?) (As she?) You just wait until I get a celebrity best friend, join their entourage, and never have to worry about money again! By the way, I didn't say that I would become a celebrity and make my own money, because I possess humility, unlike fucking Perfect Laura.

Also, Mom, if you're reading this, I'm not gay. I just don't have a boyfriend—yet. When I'm in the celebrity entourage, I'm sure I'll have boyfriends all over the place! Probably ones that have sex with my celebrity best friend! Boyfriends, three at a time! Doing it in hot tubs, on private jets, and ironically in dive-bar bathrooms! So there!

I'm sorry that I yelled just now. Which brings me to my next chapter.

GUILT
I Feel Bad for Writing
This Chapter

Sometimes I feel guilty if I slam the door too hard, not because I think it's disturbing my neighbors, but because I think that I might have hurt the door. This anthropomorphizing of doors has led me to never be able to make a final point when kicking a person out of my apartment. If I yell at someone, "And stay out!" and push them out the door, I then have to gently close it shut in their face, thus confusing the person I really and truly never want to see again into thinking that I don't really mean it. I swear I do. I just feel bad about the door.

— "Walker"

Guilt. You feel it every day when you "forget" to recycle or when your neighbor drops by unexpectedly and finds you watching *What a Girl Wants*, starring Amanda Bynes, instead of the State of the Union address. How are you to explain to them Amanda Bynes's ineffable "it" quality, which makes it impossible to tear your eyes off her charming face, whereas the excessive fawning over the president during the State of the Union gives you second-hand embarrassment? Congress is full of kiss-asses—they should have a little shame—whereas, ironically, Amanda Bynes's lack of inhibition makes her a joy to watch.

You also use guilt as a powerful tool against your child in order to keep them in line through a series of passive-aggressive psychological games designed to keep them in a state of perpetual anxiety. These games place them in a sort of emotional purgatory where they know that you are unfairly making them feel guilty but they still feel that guilt anyway, leading to a psychological stew of resentment *and* guilt. The more common term for this is "mind-fucking."

Mind-fucking is an age-old method, created by the Phoenicians as a bartering tool. They would make the Maltese second-guess the value of their wares, which were very well made, by essentially implying that the Maltese were charging too much for ceramic pots. The Phoenicians would make their eyes tear up ever so slightly so it looked like they were about to weep, but never actually would. Then they would exchange their own shoddy products, poorly constructed terra cotta, for the Maltese merchants quality ones—ivory boxes and amulets in addition to ceramic pots—and although the Maltese suspected the unfair trade, they were too mind-fucked to substantiate it, blinded as they were by the fact that they had almost made the Phoenicians cry. That is why today's actors and jerks are direct descendants of the Phoenicians, and why craftsmen and idiots are of a Maltese background.

As a parent, however, you seem to have an innate ability to make your child feel guilty. Most of the time, you're not even trying. It just comes that easily to you. You sort of imply that you would like to spend more time with them when they come to town, that maybe their friends would like to come over to your house for a drink instead of going to What's-his-face's house. You understand that What's-his-face has "cool" parents whom your child actually likes to play drinking games with, but you can be a "cool" parent, too, even if your child does think you're boring. Oh, I know they don't say that you're boring, but why else would they not have their friends come over? Oh, no, you're not trying to make them feel guilty. "Go on, get out of here!" you say. "Don't worry about leaving me alone in the house. I like my alone time. It gives me time to think about my child, even if I can't be with them when they're only home for two days."

The worst part about the guilt that you put on your child is that no matter how well they are able to withstand guilt trips from friends, significant others, and bosses who have an overly strict sense of "being on time," they will never be able to resist the guilt that you pour onto them. It truly is your greatest weapon, and hopefully there will be studies done soon in laboratories wherein they will concoct an antidote that can be taken in pill or liquid form, or as a chip implanted at the base of their spine, to withstand the force of the guilt you are able to make them feel. Therefore, since guilt really is your most powerful asset when it comes to your child, well, that and money, you are required to use it sparingly and responsibly, whereas you should use your money on your child excessively and wantonly. For example, instead of making your child feel guilty that they are going to the movies with their friend, instead of watching television with you at home, by sighing loudly and mentioning that your neighbor's children are always doing fun things with them whenever they come home, like family horseshoe tournaments, you should throw them one to two hundred dollars (and a diamond bracelet) and tell them to have a great time. The fact that you're giving them such an excessive amount of money for a movie shows how much you love them. Also, you should not want to have a child that enjoys family horseshoe tournaments, as that is a really lame way to spend time with your grown child.

Here is a list of guilt-free activities that you can participate in with your child:

1. Eating of guilt-free cookies
2. Baking and subsequent eating of guilt-free brownie cake
3. Reading a cookbook full of guilt-free recipes
4. Collaborating on the writing of a cookbook of guilt-free recipes

That is it.

THERAPY
Stop Talking About It, Crazy

My therapist told me that my dream about riding a polar bear underwater signified that I was coping with the loss of my father by escaping into fantasy. I didn't tell her that I've had a pet polar bear since age eight, when I was bequeathed one by the wizard who lived in the west wing of our castle in the Rhineland. So I stopped seeing her, because she's dead wrong about everything.

— "Sarah"

Therapy may or may not be a good idea for your child, depending on who their therapist is, and if they actually need it. If you encourage your child to go into therapy when they are actually a very happy, well-adjusted person, for which you can take much of the credit, you may cause them to second-guess their happiness, and send them into a spiral of self-doubt, which they can discuss with their therapist. The irony of this is that you were trying to cover all of your bases of being a good parent and admitting that you may have had some faults in the raising of your child, except that you didn't, until the very moment when you recommended therapy, which implied that you did. DO YOU SEE WHAT YOU'RE DOING TO ME, MOTHER????!!!

Ahem.

Many people who go to therapy like to talk about going to therapy. This is an exceptionally annoying trait, along the lines of telling tall people how tall they are. It's like, they know that they're tall, you don't have to tell them. I mean, I go to therapy, but I wouldn't write about how I, personally, go to therapy, even though there's nothing wrong with the act of seeing a therapist. It's just that people shouldn't talk about it like it's some sort of accomplishment. As long as we're on the subject, though, I really have made a lot of progress over the past year. I mean, you would not believe how many breakthroughs I've had. And I've cried, oh, yes, I've cried, and I'm not afraid to admit it. Maybe if I were a dude I'd feel weirder about saying that, but girls cry all the time, right? It doesn't mean I'm crazy. I'm just letting my feelings out, and maybe you should consider therapy, too, if you want to better yourself as a parent. However, there are some risks involved with going to a therapist—namely, sounding like a huge asshole when you talk about therapy to anyone who will listen.[1]

There are a couple of ways in which people talk about therapy. They can refer to it in sort of a defiant way, as in, "Well, I have to go to therapy later (*pause for dramatic effect, daring the other person to think that they're crazy*) ... so can we meet at the iPod store this evening? Oh, sorry, that was my other friend that I was meeting at the iPod store. I forgot. *We're* meeting

---

[1] Again, I'm not the asshole in this situation. I didn't even talk about therapy for that long. Plus, it's my book, I'll do whatever I want.

for coffee." If you have a child who would say something like that to a friend just to let their friend know that they go to therapy *and* have an iPod (which isn't such a big deal, but clearly your child thinks that it is), you have a Double Asshole (DA) on your hands, and you should seriously consider taking them out of therapy so they don't think they're such a big goddamn deal. By the way, you'd have the power to take them out of therapy, because, again, clearly you are footing the bill.

Another way people talk about therapy is when they spew out what they've learned in their last session to the unwilling listener who didn't ask for this. No, they don't think the other person sounds smart. In fact, therapy sounds like bullshit. The only person who has the ability to talk about therapy in an interesting way is Woody Allen, so if you are not Woody Allen, you are delusional if you think that I care what your therapist had to say about needing to take care of my inner child. I don't even like children (an issue I've discussed with my therapist). But look at me, being all Woody Allen and talking about therapy. No, no, *I'm* not Woody Allen, I was just acting like him just now. You didn't notice? Well, maybe you haven't seen enough of his movies.

I would not recommend going to therapy with your child. It impedes the process when the person who you want to talk most about is sitting directly beside you. I suppose that this works in couples therapy, or so I assume from watching the many romantic comedies starring Kate Hudson that have dealt with the subject. However, I can't imagine that it would not be awkward, especially with a Freudian therapist, to hash out the details of how exactly it is that all of the angst between you and your child is a result of their latent desire to sleep with you. Excuse me.

Gross.

If one takes therapy with a grain of salt and recognizes it as a helpful exercise instead of the end-all and the be-all of personal growth, then it can be a very enlightening process. There is a slight chance that your child causes you a certain amount of stress, and attending therapy may be a constructive tool to vent these frustrations without doing anything rash like cutting them off or something. If you denied your child monetary funds, you would have to be immediately confined to an insane asylum, as to leave your own flesh and blood high and dry like that could only indicate a serious mental illness. Also, you wouldn't be confined to a new, clean hospital. Your child would somehow find an old-timey haunted insane asylum, full of ghosts who died from shock therapy. Wouldn't you prefer normal therapy to shock therapy? Good, so don't cut them off. I'm not threatening you, but I just want to let you know what might happen. No, it's a guarantee. I know of three cases myself in which stingy parents have been confined to the old house on the hill next to the sleepy hollow with the haunting of the others and poltergeists in Amityville with ghostbusters. No, I'm not just naming movies, I'm trying to save you from the Pirates of the Caribbean … ghost.

Here's the breakdown:

THERAPY=Good for releasing possible frustrations you may have with your child.

CUTTING YOUR CHILD OFF MONETARILY=Inevitable haunting from old-timey ghosts who have died from shock therapy in the very same scary insane asylum where you will be confined.

SIGNIFICANT OTHERS
The Possibility That Your Child Will Not Die Alone—Unless You Somehow Screw It Up

I brought my boyfriend home to meet my parents and everything went really well until the subject of abortion came up. My boyfriend believes in a woman's right to choose, but he said that he would be ready to be a father if we made a mistake. Then my father punched him in the face. Then I punched my boyfriend in the face for basically telling my parents that we were having premarital sex. Then my brother punched my boyfriend in the face for having sex with his sister. Then I had to break up with my boyfriend because his nose was so disfigured that I didn't want to have sex with him anymore.

— "Sar"

If your child has found another person that they would like to spend the rest of their life with, this is an incredible feat. The odds of meeting that one person who will make you happy for however long they will be married for minus a couple of unhappy years where they figure out that they don't want to be married anymore are astoundingly against everyone. That's a lot of people to sift through. It's a lot of douchebags that your daughter will date and hopefully come to her senses about and reject, and a lot of skanks that your son will date and hopefully (from his perspective) have hot skank sex with and then reject. I mean, think how many people there are in China, let alone the world. The exact number escapes me at the moment. I have it written down here somewhere. I'll find it later.[1] Point being, your child has done well for themselves, just as you, assuming you're still married, did well for yourself when you landed yourself that Smith girl/Amherst man and would listen to jazz music while holding hands in the back of your Model T or whatever you crazy kids did back in the day. Therefore, it falls upon you, as the parent, to not fuck up your child's relationship. They will do that well enough on their own, as they discovered when they told their serious girlfriend while on a romantic getaway on Valentine's Day in Napa that they didn't believe in marriage. This was especially hurtful to the girlfriend, as it showcased a certain type of idiocy on the boyfriend's part, because who doesn't "believe" in marriage? It's an age-old proven institution. It's not like the state of marriage is a unicorn and he doesn't believe in unicorns. Ironically enough, the boyfriend did believe in unicorns, and although as a couple they got over the marriage dispute, it was his fervent belief in the existence of unicorns that was ultimately their undoing.

As I said, you need to be as supportive of your child in their relationships as you possibly can, up to a point,

---

[1] I looked it up on the Internet just now and apparently the Chinese population is increasing by ten million people a year and will peak in the middle of the twenty-first century at 1.6 billion.

of course. If your child's significant other is abusive, you have the right to cave in their ankles and torture them in a sort of *Misery*-type scenario, staying true to the Kathy Bates character, except instead of saying "I'm your biggest fan" you can say "I'm going to fuck you up good," which will make them tremble in fear, in addition to the uncontrollable sobbing brought about by their caved-in ankles.

If your child's significant other is way too into alcohol and/or drugs, you may also intervene and confiscate all of their drugs and drug paraphernalia, then hand them over to your child so that they may experience for themselves their harmful effects. It's the equivalent of that time when your child was thirteen and you discovered them smoking a cigarette on the corner with their then boyfriend/girlfriend who was "bad news" and you made them smoke an entire pack of cigarettes just to show them how disgusting it was. That was a good lesson. Your child never touched a cigarette again and still spontaneously vomits at the smell of cigarette smoke. You may want to be more careful in this drug situation, however, as I hear some of the drugs on the street these days are pretty addictive. You don't want your child telling everyone in rehab that you're the one that got them hooked on blow because you made them snort an entire bag of cocaine just to show them how bad it was. Plus, the weight loss as a result of their coke habit might prove to be too desirable to quit just yet, because if they are going to break up with their cokehead significant other, it wouldn't hurt to rope in someone else by looking their thinnest.

When you meet your child's hopefully relatively normal, nonabusive, non-drug-addled significant other, you must exude friendliness, but don't immediately welcome them into the family, as you don't want to make your child uncomfortable. I would suggest a screening of *Guess Who's Coming to Dinner*, the 1967 classic film starring Spencer Tracy, Katharine Hepburn, and Sidney Poitier, before you meet your child's significant other, as a guide to knowing how not to initially react, whether they be a different race from your child or no. Also, isn't it crazy how people used the term "colored" all over the place back then? Jeez.

Anyway, if you don't specifically have a *Guess Who's Coming to Dinner* scenario, you should try to avoid interactions such as this one:

YOU: (*Shoving your child out of the way and embracing their* SIGNIFICANT OTHER *in an uncomfortably long hug.*) Welcome to our home! I hope it's something like the home you will share with my child in the near future!

SIGNIFICANT OTHER: (*Politely laughing and disengaging themselves from your grip.*) Well, we've only been dating for a couple of months. I don't know if we're thinking about moving in together.

YOU: Well, I was talking about getting married, not just moving in together!

YOUR CHILD: Please stop.

SIGNIFICANT OTHER'S INNER THOUGHTS: This seals it. I am definitely breaking up as soon as we leave.

However, be wary of going in the opposite direction:

YOU: (*Stiffly extending a hand.*) Nice to meet you, (*Significant Other's Name*).

SIGNIFICANT OTHER: Nice to meet you, too.

YOU: I would offer you a chair, but I have no idea how long you two will be together.

YOUR CHILD: That was rude.

SIGNIFICANT OTHER'S INNER THOUGHTS: Yes, rude. But a good point. I am definitely breaking up when we leave.

If you meet them at a restaurant, the no-drinking rule is temporarily waived. You may all engage in cocktails, but no more than two cocktails each, and of course they may not be tequila-based, e.g., margaritas, tequila gimlets, or Juanito's Temptations. You should never drink that anyway. At any rate, there is the perfect point of tipsiness that encourages conversation but not to the point that you reveal too many details of your child's life. Here is an example of a conversation and its aftermath. It goes horribly awry because of your drunken indiscretion. I will write it in the form of a play as well, as I suspect that I am a very good playwright, as evidenced by the above examples.

Cast

YOU: The mother.

LANCE: The son.

SIMONE: The girlfriend.

DAN: The stoner friend.

DIERDRE: Ex-girlfriend, only mentioned. Smells like cereal.

Open on a dinner table at a fancy restaurant with YOU, LANCE, *and* SIMONE.

YOU: I'm so glad that you two are together now. Lance's last girlfriend wasn't very bright. Or attractive. I also think she smelled like cereal.

LANCE: Don't talk about Dierdre like that, or Simone will think that you'll talk like that about her one day.

SIMONE: I wasn't thinking that. Are we breaking up?

LANCE: No! I'm just saying—

YOU: (*Pouring yourself some more Merlot.*) Simone, what an interesting name. So, tell me, Simone, why do your parents hate America?

SIMONE: Wha—no, they don't hate America! Why do you say that?

YOU: Your name is French.

SIMONE: It was my grandmother's name.

YOU: I'm sure it was. Anyway, Simone, has Lance ever told you about the time he and his little friends performed "One" from *A Chorus Line* at his third-grade talent show?

LANCE: No! Stop!

SIMONE: (*Thinking: "That sounds gay."*) I'd love to hear it!

YOU: (*Sip.*) Lance simply *loved A Chorus Line* as a child. He watched the film almost every day for a year. He especially loved the role of Beatrice Ann "Bebe" Benson, as played in the film by the wonderful Nicole Fosse.

LANCE: Michelle Johnston.

YOU: (*Sip.*) What, dear?

LANCE: Michelle Johnston! Michelle Johnston played the role of Beatrice Ann "Bebe" Benson. Nicole Fosse played Kristine Evelyn Erlich-DeLuca!

SIMONE: (*Thinking.*) Oh God.

YOU: Yes, of course, Lance. (*Sip.*) *Anyway*, Lance and his two little girlfriends performed "One" in front of the entire school! I made them gold sequined vests and shorts and they had little gold top hats and tap shoes. Wait! I think I have a picture!

(*Pulls out picture.*)

SIMONE: That's adorable!

LANCE: Yep, that's it. Moving on—

YOU: (*Sip.*) So! The point comes in the finale where Lance and his friends are doing a high-kick line and suddenly Lance stops and runs offstage! No one knew what had happened, but it turns out that he had pooped his pants!

LANCE *starts uncontrollably coughing.*

SIMONE: (*Thinking: "Gross."*) Huh.

YOU: (*Sip.*) I actually have a video of it as well.

LANCE: (*Recovering himself.*) Stop drinking right now.

Cut to six months later. SIMONE *and* LANCE *are now broken up after* LANCE*'s infidelity.* LANCE *receives a phone call from his friend* DAN.

DAN: Dude. Simone has a blog.

LANCE: So?

DAN: Um. It's called Lanceshitshispants.blogspot. It tells some story about how you shit your pants when you were in *A Chorus Line* when you were twenty-one?

LANCE: I was eight!

DAN: Either way, *A Chorus Line*? Are you gay?

LANCE: No, I cheated on Simone, for God's sake!

DAN: With a dude?

LANCE: No!

DAN: Either way, her blog has like twelve thousand hits already. And a link to your mom's website, www.lances-momandbestfriend.com, where she tells the same story, but with a picture and a video.

LANCE: I need to go.

DAN: Why, do you have a guy over or something?

LANCE: No!

LANCE *angrily hangs up, puts face in hands.*

END SCENE.

Wow, that was really good. I might make that into a full-length play. It will be titled *A Chorus Line*—no … it will be called *Les Misérables*.

Let's assume that at some point you will meet the person that your child is committed to and they have decided to become engaged. You will probably be very pleased at this news, considering that this means grandchildren aren't very far away. Actually, they may be currently on the way, because, let's be honest, the couple is a bit young and why do you think they're so anxious to get married right away? People don't normally get married in January, one month after getting engaged, and don't you find it a bit suspect that they're registered at Babies 'R' Us? No matter. Point is, I'm sure they love each other, so much so that they would have sex before marriage. (BURN IN HELL, DIRTY FORNICATORS!!!)

Baby or no, either way, you have a wedding to attend … and pay for. If your daughter is getting married, it is traditionally your job to fund the wedding, and that can be the cause of a significant amount of stress, as we all learned in the hilarious 1991 comedy *Father of the Bride*, starring Steve Martin as George Stanley Banks, the stingy, anxious, yet ultimately loving dad, and Kimberly Williams as Annie Banks, his cloying daddy's-girl daughter. Did anyone else notice that she got married at twenty-one in the movie and she hadn't even graduated college, as she met

Bryan MacKenzie during her junior year abroad in Rome? I'm sure in the 1950 original this was perfectly acceptable, but I think that perhaps the filmmakers should have thought of the social implications of that move. If Annie wanted to be an architect so badly, why didn't she and Bryan at least live together first? And, furthermore, why did she get so upset over the blender incident? Because she thought that it implied that she was a '50s housewife? Isn't she essentially succumbing to 1950s norms by marrying at such a young age without thinking of her career? I realize this point is made by Steve Martin in the movie, but Diane Keaton points out that when they were married they had never lived together, but still, things were different then, and I don't think that that's a basis for comparison. I believe that the filmmakers were trying to have it both ways by adhering to the spirit of the original while glossing over the realities of the double standard imposed on a modern-day woman to pursue both a career and a family. Furthermore, the whole basketball scene the night before the wedding is totally wrong. If they used to play basketball so much together, maybe George could have taught Annie some form. She shoots with two hands, for God's sakes. And then it snows? Are you fucking kidding me? Are we supposed to suspend so much disbelief that in addition to believing that it snows in L.A. we also think that a guy who owns a Porsche and a huge house in an obviously affluent suburb would scrimp over a nice wedding *and* fall for Martin Short's ridiculous accent?? COME ON, HOLLYWOOD! AND FOR SHAME, STEVE MARTIN!

But I digress. You would be lucky if you emulated Steve Martin in any way, even if you made a series of crappy movies, which I can only assume you agreed to so that you could fund your extensive and ever-growing collection of contemporary art and be able to support yourself as a writer of lightly humorous and intelligent yet mildly heartbreaking novellas, which, after all, is your true passion. Point being, offer as little input and resistance to wedding plans as is possible. You may draw the line at fireworks that spell out the newlyweds' names, for instance, but please do not force them to buy the "Cookie Puss" cake from Carvel because you enjoy your cake in the shape of a cat with the tiny cookie crumbles that act as crust on the bottom. Yes, everyone loves ice-cream cake. No one is arguing with you there. However, there is a time and a place for ice-cream cake—specifically, every occasion in which a cake is required except for weddings.

HERE ARE THE EVENTS AT WHICH AN ICE-CREAM CAKE IS AN ACCEPTABLE TYPE OF CAKE:

Children's Birthday Parties

Adult Birthday Parties

Going-Away Parties

Welcome-Home Parties

Opening-Night Parties

Wrap Parties

Lame Office Parties

Fun Office Parties

Fun "Let's Have a Cake Because We Want One and It's Summer" Parties

Fun "Pretend Like It's Summer and Let's Have an Ice-Cream Cake Even Though It's Snowing" Parties

"I Express My Emotions via Ice-Cream Cake" Parties

"We Love Ice-Cream Cake" Parties

"We Hate Ice-Cream Cake So We'll Eat It Ironically" Parties

HERE ARE THE EVENTS AT WHICH AN ICE-CREAM CAKE IS NOT AN ACCEPTABLE TYPE OF CAKE:

Weddings

A Message from the Author

Listen, I'd like to take off my advice-giving sweater vest, sit backwards in a chair, and just rap with you for a few. How are you doing? You know what? In case you are still having doubts as to my advice-giving prowess, here are some more things that you should know about me, because I'm just a person, much like yourself, whom you can totally trust.

1. **I ENJOY DRINKING BEER.** This means that I am both down-to-earth and not afraid of a few calories, much like I am not afraid of telling it like it is, in a smooth, ice-cold, hops-y manner.

2. **I HAVE TWO OLD JANE FONDA WORKOUT RECORDS FRAMED IN MY APARTMENT.** Both of them sport Jane Fonda on the cover in a leotard and leggings and leg warmers in various nonstrenuous workout positions. This means that I am open to working out *problems*, in a stylish manner.

3. **I LIVE NEXT TO A BOOKSTORE CALLED BIOGRAPHY, WHICH DOES NOT CARRY A COPY OF**

THE BIBLE. Trust me, I've asked them. When I pointed out that the Bible is the biography of Jesus Christ, they laughed. Though I know that I am clearly in the right on this front, and have every right to boycott them, I still go in there, because I am tolerant of all peoples and religions, much like Jesus Christ.

4. **SOMETIMES I DATE ACTORS, AND THIS IS A TERRIBLE IDEA.** This advice is not related to this book, but if you're a single parent, or a single person in general, I recommend not dating an actor. If you're an actor, don't call me, because I won't date you. So there.

Okay, enough about me! I'm going to re-don my advice-giving sweater vest and sit in my chair frontwards, like a normal person.

REHEARSAL DINNER
Par ... ty?

My mom had lost her voice the day before my rehearsal dinner, so during her speech she whispered to my dad and he said it for everyone to hear. I realize now that this could have been one of the factors that led up to their divorce, as I'm almost positive that my mom would never say, "I hope that my child is a far better wife than I, as I have never lifted a finger to help my husband in our entire thirty years of marriage, even when he asked nicely."

— "Winston"

W e have reached the endgame. Your child is about to get married. Technically, you can still keep fucking them up, but you are now out of my jurisdiction. I am trying to help your lamentably unmarried offspring through the period of being single in the eyes of God.[1] Once they become joined with another person, that person assumes much of the fucking-up responsibility, with some help from their in-laws. Please, though, let us not stoop to in-law jokes. I think we like each other too much for

---

[1] Unless they're gay, and apparently they'll always be single in the eyes of God until some crazy liberal artsy-fartsy president feels like giving them basic human rights.

that. It should be noted, though, that you will be an in-law once your child is married, so you may direct any strong desires to fuck someone up toward your child's spouse, the results of which will indirectly reach your child.

Remember, though, until the minister or rabbi or recently online-ordained officiator pronounces them man and wife, they are still single, and you still have the ability, nay, almost perverse desire, to continue to directly fuck them up. You must learn to harness this desire.

It's much like when you were hooking up with that British exchange student back in college and you knew that they were bad news but since they were leaving forever in December you figured, "The hell with it, I'm going to spend as much time as possible with this person, and if I get hurt, I'll deal with that later."

Well, you were wrong, my friend. So very, very wrong. Now you are grown up and your child has taken the place of that British exchange student, and although they lack the charming accent and dry wit, they are still leaving you. Leaving you hurt and alone and with a slight fear of disease, though for different reasons. Therefore, you must gradually pull yourself away from your child, realizing that the end point is near and that your relationship is about to drastically change. For example, if your child were that British exchange student, you would start screening their calls sometime around early November and probably choose not to sleep with them for a month before their departure. Yes, it's exactly like that.

WHAT YOUR CHILD SHOULD DO

As you are well aware, the process of getting married, if done in the traditional sense, is very costly and time-consuming. If your child has any sense at all, they will elope with their fiancé(e) and then whisk away to some exotic locale, preferably a politically unstable tropical isle or one of those Central American countries that have become so popular these days. This will provide them with more interesting stories when they return. No one wants to hear about the seafood tower served at the Sandals resort in Jamaica. What we want to know about is how they accidentally ended up in a defunct hotel, now brothel, in Panama City, Panama, or fighting alongside the Sandinistas in Nicaragua. You would do well to encourage them in this direction, as it saves you the expense of both the wedding and the honeymoon, since the nightly price of a brothel cannot be beat. In an ideal scenario, your child will elope and have an adventure with their new spouse in Belize wherein they obtain, through a series of lucky accidents and planned heists, an ancient Mayan artifact. Although the artifact is beautiful and priceless, they will do the honorable thing and return it to its rightful owner, Josephina, the whore with the heart of gold who has been wallowing in the brothel where they are staying. She may now return to her large family estate in the mountains, having regained her birthright, recovered by your child and their spouse. She will be eternally grateful and they will spend the remainder of their stay on her sprawling estate where peacocks roam free. They will then return home triumphantly and throw a huge Mayan-themed party in celebration of their new life together.

However, if your child desires a more "traditional" wedding, you will have to submit to a series of rituals far more painful and difficult than the cannibalistic ceremonies of the indigenous people of Belize.

WHAT YOUR CHILD WILL PROBABLY DO

Your child will probably opt for the more traditional wedding, which is too bad, since when are they ever going to see Belize? However, that's their choice, isn't it? Therefore, we begin with the rehearsal dinner.

The rehearsal dinner is generally thrown by the groom's parents and is an intimate affair, as it is only for members of the wedding party and the immediate family. It is also a chance for whoever feels the urge to give a speech to do so. This is especially dangerous, as, unlike the wedding, there is no limit on how many people can give a speech. Even if people hadn't planned on speaking, the urge to clink a fork against a glass is just too powerful and they find themselves doing it and then realizing that they have nothing to say. Speeches at the wedding are relegated to the parents and the best man and the maid of honor, so the rehearsal dinner is when the crazies really get to come out of the woodwork, i.e., Uncle Derek, who takes this opportunity to out himself to the family. Let's be honest, though: We all knew he was gay. Even Granny knew that "confirmed bachelor" was a euphemism for "closeted gay." Anyway, even the completely innocuous speeches tend to ramble, as the guests take advantage of the free booze, as anyone would. However, free booze coupled with close family, as we already know, leads to disaster. Therefore, you would do well to have a cutoff point on the champagne or Prosecco or whatever sparkling beverage you provided. Yes, this may anger some guests, but they will thank you later when they realize the embarrassment that you spared them, as at the next open-bar rehearsal dinner that they attend they'll think it's funny when they perform a striptease for the horrified non-English-speaking Argentinean cousin of the bride.

REHEARSAL-DINNER SPEECHES

When it comes to your speech, keep it short, simple, and complimentary. Please refrain from jokes. I can tell you right now, you're not funny. Compliment the bride and groom, say what lovely people they are and that you know they'll be very happy together, choke back some tears, take a moment, then raise your glass and "Cheers!" This should take no more than a minute and a half. Someone should actually be timing you with a stopwatch, and if you go over the minute-and-a-half mark, they should have the authority to tackle you, use a shepherd's hook to drag you offstage, or simply shoot you with a tranquilizer gun. The very worst thing you could do is use your speech as some sort of roast of the happy couple. It is very difficult to endearingly and humorously make fun of someone when you lack the subtle comedic chops of Jimmy Kimmel.

An Example of an Acceptable Rehearsal-Dinner Speech

If I could have everyone's attention for just a moment … Please, please, keep drinking, it'll only help me sound funny. *(Pause for laughter.)* See? Tommy, could you please start the stopwatch, I don't want to go over a minute and a half. Started? Great, then I'll get on with it! I'd like to raise a glass to the bride and groom and just say what you all already know, that this is an exceptional couple who make me proud every minute of the day, so proud that I'd like to take this opportunity to announce that I am going to pay for their honeymoon! First-class airfare, five-star hotel, meals, everything! And some spending money—don't forget to bring us home a souvenir! Just kidding, keep it all for yourselves, I will be ANGRY if you spend more than twenty-five cents on a postcard for me! That's right, kids, this is just a little gift from me to say, well, to say … *(Pause to wipe eyes/ choke back tears.)* To say … thank you … for being you. *(Pause for everyone else to cry a little, then raise glass.)* To the bride and groom.

An Example of a Terrible Rehearsal-Dinner Speech

If I could have everyone's attention! Hey! Everyone! *(Rings cowbell.)* Ha! Thought I'd need this! I said, hey, I think I'm gonna NEED MORE COWBELL!! Haha! Before I talk about the lovely couple, who, by the way, I expect to reimburse me in FULL for this little soiree, haha, I'd like to try out some standup I've been working on, now that I have your attention. You can say you saw it here first!

It's just ten minutes, don't worry. Now, folks, don't you think it's weird that women get really annoying around a certain time of the month? Fellas, you know what I'm talking about … *(Nine and half minutes later.)* … and I said, "Two gays? More like gaze!" See, folks, that was a pun. Ah, thank you all for indulging me. I'll tell the wait staff to start serving wine again soon. I just didn't want any distractions for you all! You know how annoying waiters can be! So, in all seriousness, I'd like to say I'm so happy that these kids found each other. At the very least, it must be a relief for them, knowing now that they won't die alone, unless they divorce! You kids signed a prenup, right? Great. Anyway, enough about them. If you want to hear more of my standup, I'll be right over here with the booze! Haha! So raise your water glasses, and let's toast to the bride and groom!

POST-REHEARSAL-DINNER

After the rehearsal dinner, you can all go to the local bar and get hammered if that's your thing, but you'll probably have to take care of Uncle Derek, who is now regretting his decision to out himself in such a manner. Just reassure him that he had by far the most interesting speech of the dinner, and, as delicately as you can, imply that this was no big surprise. Also, you should be grateful to Uncle Derek, since he made the biggest fuckup of the evening, which distracted from the fact that you thought it would be fun to key cars in the parking lot with your nineteen-year-old nephew. Don't worry, that won't be awkward next time you see him … which will be the next day at the wedding, where he'll act overly familiar toward you because now he thinks that you're friends, on par with his college buddies, and that you'll play *Madden* and eat Tostitos until 5 A.M. on a Monday night together. You might consider snubbing him, figuring that he'll amount to nothing anyway. Yes, this may hurt his feelings, but it will make it easier for you to deny the incident to his parents. In fact, you'll probably tell his parents that you caught him keying cars in the parking lot as opposed to participating in the keying of cars with him. Yes, this has the potential to intensely fuck your nephew up, but at least it's not your child, and that's the most important thing.

WEDDING:
It's Official. Your Child Will Not Die Alone. Unless They Divorce or Their Spouse Dies First, But You Know What I Mean.

At my sister's wedding this was my father's speech: "We're all very proud of Laura. She is at the top of her med school class, can speak five different languages and is a loving, caring person. Jim is very lucky to have married her. Jim is also an 'actor.' And Jewish. Anyway. I love my daughter.

— "S. W. W."

Once you have made it through the rehearsal dinner it's time for the wedding. You thought that you were an emotional wreck at the rehearsal dinner? Well, as the Bachman-Turner Overdrive so wonderfully put it in their number-one *Billboard* hit of 1974: You ain't seen nothing yet. Of course, you will have a strong emotional upsurge when you see your child getting married, but please refrain from spontaneous sickness as caused by emotional instability, such as hysterical blindness or the sudden loss of the power of speech or hearing. No one wants Helen Keller at their wedding. Well, maybe the actual Helen Keller would have been nice to have around, since she was a genius and whatnot, but you as Helen Keller is so not cool. There can only be one Helen Keller.

Just try to keep calm. Remember that this is a joyous occasion. Well, hopefully it's a joyous occasion and your child hasn't fallen in love with a prisoner through what started off as a harmless pen-pal relationship and now, six months later, here you are, watching your child marry an inmate as they press their hands together through Plexiglas. Whether the wedding's in a church or in a federal detention center, you might want to consider using some breathing exercises. These breathing exercises should be subtle, not loud and Lamaze-like, which would interrupt the vows—even if the vows are really lame because they were written by the couple. Well, if your child is marrying the prisoner, maybe it wouldn't be the worst thing in the world to loudly breathe over their self-written vows, especially the "I promise to take a shiv to whoever looks at you cockeyed" vow.

Keep focused and ignore the distractions around you. Now is not the time to realize that you said dove-white flowers, not egg-white flowers goddamn it, and start seething inside to the point of flinging the prayer book at the egg-white flowers. People may think that this indicates a disapproval of the wedding ceremony, as opposed to the gradation in white of the flowers. People might think that you're nuts, but little do they know. It's just about flower professionalism and the total inappropriate nature of egg-white over dove-white at a wedding and anyone can see this, okay??

Look at the happy couple and reflect on nothing but them. Do not start to think about your failed relationships. Do not look over to see your ex happily sitting, holding hands with their new significant other, and then realize that your date is newly gay Uncle Derek. Do not try to consider what this might mean, that perhaps you are in a bad place, that perhaps it was a mistake to divorce your spouse, and how tacky is it that they showed up at your child's wedding with their significant other, whom they've only been dating for four months and who is twenty-two years their junior? Do not think that you would do the same thing, too, if your significant other were that hot. Do not think that perhaps your ex brought their exorbitantly hot significant other to the wedding solely to make you jealous and that this indicates that they really do want you back. You were, after all, married for thirty years and share two children together, one of whom is getting married at this very moment. Upon this reasoning, do not decide to make a boldly romantic gesture in the middle of the ceremony and proclaim your undying love for your ex just before the ring exchange. Do not burst into tears and tear down those damn egg-white flowers when your ex tells you, no, they do not still love you and to show a little decorum at your child's wedding. Do not try to punch their new, hot, young significant other in the neck when they wrinkle up their nose and say, "Gross," when you start to cry. Although this would be a spectacular way to fuck up your child one last time, this does not conform to the gradual-pulling-away process that I spoke of earlier. If you are truly going to taper the fucking-up-age to the point of stopping once your child says "I do," you may accidentally spill red wine on your ex's significant other later. Please do not do this in church, unless you are at a Catholic Mass and you take Communion next to the new significant other and you spit-take the Blood of Christ all over them.

If the wedding takes place at a private residence, be sure to compliment the host, because if they have a big enough house with the requisite number of fountains and naked-lady statues to host a wedding, they most likely have Mafia ties. Make a mental note to check to see how and why your child's new spouse knows someone in the Mafia. Don't make too big a deal out of it—you don't want them to think you're sticking your nose into their business. You should probably resign yourself to looking at it as a positive thing. Yes, the Mafia has a long history of violence and illegal activity, but many have lived under its protection, until they started snooping around to see if their child's spouse was connected with them and then they ended up with the fishes. That is, they lost their job as a highly paid lawyer and had to find employment as a fishmonger. You hate fish, even fancy sushi. So just let it go.

In terms of gifts for the bride and groom, as the parent, you should feel free to stray from the registry and give them something truly unique and special. It should be something that will turn into an heirloom, but not an old-timey heirloom like a wreath of ancestral hair, which is both creepy and gross. Perhaps something like a solid-gold croquet set with the family crest emblazoned on every ball. If you don't have a family crest, you could create one. This will show off your artistic skills and create an air of aristocracy around your family, distracting from the fact that you are descendants of early coal miners in West Virginia. That is obviously nothing to be ashamed of, and you can render lumps of coal and pickaxes into the family crest, but due to the tiny nature of the crest on the croquet balls, the coal and pickaxes will look like royal orbs and scepters, and you should not disabuse people of this.

At this point, give yourself a little credit. You may pat yourself on the back and congratulate yourself on a job well done on raising your child to the point where they are willing to care about another person to such an extent that they are even willing to go through the process of planning and executing a wedding. Yes, this person may just be using them to get a green card, but your child may actually feel something like love, mostly because they like their accent.

PREGNANCY
Eegs!

As of this writing, I am not pregnant. At least, I don't think so. Shit.

— "Sarah W. Walker"

Following the rule that twenty-eight is the new twenty-one, it's slightly uncomfortable that your child is either pregnant or has impregnated someone whilst in their twenties. More often than not, they are not ready to have a kid, even though they may draw solace from thinking about how in olden times ages thirteen to fifteen were the prime childbearing years. You might want to remind them that those people lived to be about thirty-five at best.

Well, maybe they do want to have a kid and they have been happily married for five years somehow. Jerks. However, if this is an unplanned pregnancy, you can make them feel better by reminding them that putting artificial substances in your body, such as birth control, or unnatural synthetics on your body, such as condoms, is really ultimately more harmful to their health than having an adorable baby! Here are some more tips on how to show support to your freaked-out son[1] or daughter.

---

[1] Obviously, your son is not pregnant, unless you've entered some sort of *Junior* situation, *Junior* being the film starring Arnold Schwarzenegger and

1. Remind them that you had them when you were twenty-five and in your third year of law school, *during* exams. So if they'd like to go to law school and complete it in the next nine months and build a successful career, instead of being an "artist," that would be more than okay with you. You know what? That's really not advice. You don't have to rub that one in.

2. Having babies as early as possible is a good thing, because global warming is progressing at such an escalated rate that they'll want to know your child for as long as possible before we all melt into the sea.

3. Their friends will thank your child for improving their social life. When they all go out to the bars together, your child can smuggle their baby in, and this tiny new member of the crew will have girls lining up to speak to their guy friends and guys will be fascinated by how much beer the baby can drink, will want a baby of their own, and will take home your child's girlfriends as a consequence.

4. Remember that weird dancing baby from that show *Ally McBeal*? Or if you didn't watch Ally McBeal, did you watch *I Love the '90s* where they discuss the creepy dancing baby? Well, assure your child that real babies look nothing like that and don't dance, so don't worry. Also, their baby will have nothing to do with *I Love the*

Emma Thompson where Schwarzenegger is pregnant (really, Emma Thompson?), which in that case they should be totally freaked out. No, just if your son has impregnated somebody and is freaked, though I'm sure he is taking full responsibility and being super-awesome to his girl-friend/wife. Right?? Right.

'90s, so they can rest doubly assured. Also, Vonda Shepard will not provide the soundtrack to their baby's life, à la *Ally McBeal*. You know what? Just tell them that their baby's life will not be affected by or similar in any way to *Ally McBeal* or *I Love the '90s* and they will be free from worry.

5. Babies will ultimately become adults who will continuously accuse them of fucking them up, yet in the same breath will demand rent money. Isn't that awesome?

SO YOU'RE A CELEBRITY
Don't Read This If
You're Not a Celebrity

Call me: 646-555-1802
—Sarah Winston Walker, author of this book

First, let me just say that I love your work. I know you don't like people to bother you, but, you know, I'm kind of a celebrity like you, now that I have a book, so it's cool. Anyway, like I said, I'm a huge fan, but by virtue of you being an awesome celebrity, just as you live life in a brighter Technicolor hue than the rest of us, so have you had more opportunities to fuck up your child than the average parent. Sorry, that's just the way it is. The only exception to this rule is Meryl Streep, because she's perfect. However, if you are anyone on the celebrity list, from A to D, and if, by virtue of your fame, your child is anywhere in the public realm, they are, and are going to continue to be, extra fucked up. Again, I'm sorry, but the fact that you, because of your mild to major successes, exposed your unwitting child to the public eye before they had the chance to make the decision for themselves is very fucked up. Whether you've sold baby photos of them, cast them as a child model to shill your clothing line, used their name for your failed restaurant, or employed them as a human shield to get past the paparazzi, you have traded in good parenting for your career. That's cool, a lot of people do it, but you're a celebrity, for God's sake. Show a little decorum. I expect it from the lawyers and the doctors of the world, who spend all of their time at work, but you, as a celebrity, are held to a higher standard.

Thank you for reading my book, by the way, and please tell your celebrity friends about it. If you want to talk about it in person, or discuss the screen adaptation of my book, you can get in touch with me through my publisher. I would publish my address here, but I don't want any noncelebrities showing up at my doorstep. Normal people are just so *nonfamous*.

Also, let me be clear: I am sure that I will dabble in celebrity upon the release of this book, which I anticipate will create a mild to major stir for its controversial overtones and general amazingness. However, I am not a parent, so if I choose to drive drunk on the left side of the road on Sunset on my way to an embarrassingly drunken interview on *Leno*, that is completely my prerogative and will affect no one but myself … and my family and fans, but you can be *sure* that neither the book sales nor my nonexistent child will suffer. Also, let me stress that I would have preferred to appear on *Letterman* or *Conan*, but, as you know, you just have to do what your publicist tells you to do. Celebrity really is a burden. Or so I anticipate.

Once you are a celebrity with a grown child, you just have to hope to God that they can make a living doing their own thing, which will probably mean trading on your name and becoming a moderate movie star or rock star in their own right. Or they could write a book about being the child of a celebrity. Any way you slice it, they're going to get by on your name. Even if they change their last name, the people in the know will know that they are your child and hire them because of this. The most famous example of this, as everyone knows, is M. Night Shyamalan's casting of Bryce Dallas Howard for the starring role in *The Village*, without an audition, after he saw her perform in a production of *As You Like It*. And it somehow slipped his mind that she is Ron Howard's daughter. Right. By the way, if any of you are thinking that I traded on my own father's name to get this book deal, you are so wrong. Sure, my father, Nicholas Walker, was on *General Hospital* from 1989 to 1990, and, yeah, he did an episode of *Melrose Place*, and, yes, he was in arguably the best Lifetime movie of all time, *Co-ed Call Girl*, but I have never and will never mention that to prospective employers or publishers or boyfriends.[1]

A FEW WORDS FROM STEPHEN WALKER, MINOR CELEBRITY AS OF A FEW SECONDS AGO

Stephen Walker here, father of published author Sarah Walker. As I am now a celebrity, I'd like to talk to the other celebrities who just finished reading the last sec-

---

[1] Nicholas Walker is not my father. I was just saying that to make a point. My father's name is Stephen Walker. Now that he's in this book, he's sort of a celebrity. And you can be sure that I will not trade on his celebrity that I created just now to get ahead. By the way, did you know that my father is Stephen Walker? He was mentioned in this book. Pretty cool, I know, having a celebrity dad. But I've made my own way.

tion. Everyone else can just tune out and turn on your television in your trailer or something. Not like a movie-set trailer, where celebrities wait in-between takes. I mean like the kind of trailer where you noncelebrities live. These past couple of seconds where I have come into my own celebrity have been quite overwhelming, so I understand where you are coming from, in that sometimes it's hard to be a celebrity and not just plain old Mom or Dad. However, as I've been a celebrity's dad longer than I've been an actual celebrity myself, I'd like to say a couple of words to those other parents of celebrities out there.

When Sarah started to write this book and anticipated her own celebrity, she became almost insufferable. She would address me like a lackey. In fact, when I finally said, "Stop treating me like your lackey," she took to the word "lackey" so much that she started to refer to me as "Lackey." I refused to respond, and we didn't speak for six months, but finally she relented and started calling me "Dad" again. Yes, she says "Dad" in a very sarcastic manner, sort of like, "Daaaaa-aaaaaad," while rolling her eyes, but it's my name nonetheless. So, my advice is, be firm with your celebrity child. Never let them forget that fame is fleeting and that it doesn't give you carte blanche to act like an asshole, especially to your parents, who brought you into this world in the first place. Now, I'm sorry, I have to go fetch Sarah a Venti Latte and a Bloody Mary. She likes to be both caffeinated and drunk when she writes, but she refuses to drink Red Bull and vodka. These crazy kids!

Daaaa-aaad. That's enough, no one cares what you think. It's true, though. I enjoy drinking lattes and Bloody Marys simultaneously. It keeps me at the top of my writing-advice game. I also enjoy drinking Bloody Marys at night, which is highly unorthodox, but we celebrities are eccentric that way. I call Bloody Marys at night "Sailor's Delight." Get it? "Red sky at night, sailor's delight"? Never mind, you have to be famous to understand it, I guess.

NOTABLE PEOPLE THROUGHOUT HISTORY WHO HAD GREAT PARENTS AND SOME OTHER PEOPLE WITH GREAT PARENTS WHOM YOU MAY NOT KNOW

NAPOLEON BONAPARTE: His parents told him that he was the only normal person in a race of genetically deficient giants. This gave him the confidence to start wars and marry and such and have an *entire* complex named after him. I'm sure that his parents gave him money, too.

ANNABELLE JENKINS (I DON'T THINK YOU KNOW HER): Her parents instilled in her the values of the 1840s, which require covering every inch of the skin and carrying a parasol. As a result, her skin is dewy and fresh as spring.

CATHERINE THE GREAT: Her parents named her "the Great." Enough said.

TODD BLACK (YOU PROBABLY DON'T KNOW HIM): His dad took him to Malaysia, where he got a tattoo from native tribesmen. This tattoo makes him incredibly sexy to the ladies and he is never lonely.

HENRY VIII: Henry had enough confidence from being an eighth that he created a religion and had six whole wives! That is, until he cut off most of their heads, and then they weren't whole anymore. (*Pause for laughter.*) His parents also made him a king, providing him with money and power and prestige.

EMILY BIGGS (MY COLLEGE ROOMMATE): She's in a band with her parents called Emily and the Biggs. They have great success traveling the country in a giant painted bus. The fact that her parents named the band after her shows a confidence in her singing-songwriting ability that has led her to produce some truly innovative music.

WOLFGANG AMADEUS MOZART: His parents combined two of the most badass words ever, "wolf" and "gang," to make his first name. Also, they gave him a tiny, tiny harpsichord when he was an infant because they knew his favorite Peanuts character was Schroeder.[2] It was this attention to their child's tastes that led to one of history's foremost musical geniuses.

LANA SULLIVAN (MAYBE YOU KNOW HER FROM THAT THING YOU WENT TO ONCE): Her parents gave her an island. This makes her happy.

---

[2] Mozart never took offense that Schroeder's favorite composer was Beethoven, because he was secure enough in his talent, as his parents were super-supportive and drove him to his harpsichord lessons every day.

J.K. ROWLING: Her parents sent her to a school for witches and wizards, where she simply transcribed everything that happened, and she went on to sell these memoirs for hundreds of millions of dollars.

GERTRUDE BRANTLEY (YOU MIGHT HAVE MET ONCE AT A PARTY): Feasts on tarts and pies that her mother still bakes for her and sends in frequent care packages. People from miles around come to share her tarts and pies and talk about life and love and literature and she is renowned for these tart-and-pie salons.

PETER DRYDEN (FRIEND FROM MY FIRST JOB): His father introduced him to the phrase "That's in my wheelhouse," which he uses to great success in job interviews. In case you don't know it, or think it's a made-up phrase, like I first did, instead of saying, "I enjoy the music of Sam Cooke," you could say, "Sam Cooke is in my wheelhouse."

NOW LET'S
ALL CRY TOGETHER

I'd like to thank you all for coming on this difficult but ultimately rewarding journey with me. Much has been said in these chapters that may frighten and confuse you. You may be asking yourself why it appears I have written the book in real time and can carry on written conversations with friends and relatives with seemingly no editing process. If that is the case, you are asking too many questions and I can have you killed. Just kidding! No, really, stop asking, just believe that I am always right and can do no wrong, which is exactly what you should make your child feel.

You may have laughed … and cried. You may have felt slightly hungry at times, and hopefully you put down the book for a second to get a healthy snack, then came right back to it.

I'd like to say a few words on how to maintain your newfound glorious relationship with your child before I leave you. Just know that you might go on a good-parenting bender right after you put this book down. However, like all benders, this will end, and you'll be left with a hangover and an empty wallet. Take it slowly. Like anything newly learned, it will take some time to adjust to your new relationship, like a new pair of crocodile boots or chinchilla gloves that would be just perfect for your child.

In the end, know that your child loves you and appreciates everything that you have done and said, but mostly what you have not done and said. I believe it was Genghis Khan who once said that actions speak more loudly than words. He may have been a jerk in some respects, but he really hit the nail on the head with that one. Incidentally, he was a parent who let his children be, and they turned out great, I assume, I really don't know. Anyway, whenever you feel the need to meddle in your child's life, think of Genghis Khan and this book and just calm down. Your child is doing great and you helped them become the capable, brilliant, attractive, literate, compassionate, idealistic, brave, popular, fun-loving person that they are today. And if they're none of these things, well, that's too bad. You might have a loser for a kid. There's nothing you, nor I, can do. I mean, they're twentysomething years old, for God's sake, let them take a little responsibility for once! Grow up! You know what would be a perfect motivator to make them grow up? Some money.

No, no, I'm sorry. You and your child have to work together, no matter what their age, because family is family and you're all you have. Now let's bring it in. C'mon. Just a little hug. There ya go. It's okay to cry.

A Message from the Author

It's me again! I feel that now our trust level has worked itself to a point where I can really open up to you. Those messages from before didn't really show you the *real* me. Well, maybe they did, but be prepared to be exposed to me in a way that I've never been exposed before! I worked out for eight months straight to bring you this full-frontal nude photo of me, so be prepared to— Excuse me.

It has just come to my attention that the naked centerfold picture of me is "in bad taste." So you can blame my publisher for that. I guess we'll just have to be a little less intimate. I don't know what I'm supposed to do with this perfectly toned body and awesome (and expensive) spray tan now. I guess I'll just have to have my own video blog or something. Anyway, that's for me to figure out.

I hope that you haven't just opened this book at random and come to this list, because, honestly, I don't really know you and I think you should read the book first like everyone else.

Are they gone? Jeez, what a jerk. Anyway, for the rest of you, as you would most likely assume, I'm feeing a bit guilty for writing this book outlining the harsh realities of parenting, especially after my parents have been so supportive of me. To make myself feel even guiltier as punishment, I thought I'd compile a list of books that my parents would have preferred that I'd written. And I'll write *all* of them right after I finish this one. I promise.

My Parents Are Awesome

How to Deal (With Too Awesome Parents)

Raised Right

How I Made My First Million at Age Twenty-One:
    A True Story

Buying Your Parents an Italian Villa for Dummies

Why My Mother Is My Best Friend:
    A Christmas Story

My Father, the Hero: An Easter Tale

My Brother Is Not in Prison; Rather, He Is One of the
    Founders of Google: For the Soul

The Devil Wears Prada

The Da Vinci Code

END-OF-THE-BOOK
SURVEY

1. What did you learn from this book?

   _____
   _____
   _____
   _____

2. How do you feel right now? You look kind of tired, and I know I hate when people say, "You look tired," but you do.

   _____
   _____
   _____
   _____

3. If you were stuck on a desert island, what five albums would you take with you?

   _____
   _____
   _____
   _____

4. Same question, but what five books?

_____

_____

_____

_____

5. Do you think I'll be more popular if this book does well? Not that I care, but do you think maybe I'll go out on more dates?

_____

_____

_____

_____

6. Between a young Orson Welles and a young Bob Dylan, who would you rather do/be friends with?

_____

_____

_____

_____

7. Would you rather have the power of flight or the power of invisibility?

_____

_____

_____

_____

About the Author

Photo by Timothy Devine

Sarah Walker is from West Hartford, Connecticut, and graduated from Amherst College in 2003 with a double degree in English and Fine Arts. During and since college she has worked as a lackey, both unpaid and slightly paid, at lots of late night television shows, most recently *The Daily Show*. She performs with her sketch comedy duo Walker and Cantrell at the Upright Citizens Brigade Theatre in New York, and has been published in *McSweeney's* online. She enjoys eating cake.

Acknowledgments

There are so many people to thank, most notably my parents, who, seriously, I cannot believe are so cool with this book. At least I think they are. I'll ask them later.

Thank you to John, my brother and my drummer.

Luanne Rice, my mentor and friend, who has provided me with immeasurable support and at least numbering in the hundreds lunches at the Half King.

John Warner, my wonderful editor, who asked me to do this book in the first place and whose very friendly rejection e-mails from McSweeneys.net encouraged me to keep submitting … and keep getting rejected. Until I didn't.

Annelise Robey, my agent, who ever so gently has made me realize that I would have no idea what I was doing were it not for her. She is SUPER good at what she does.

All of my friends: Jessie, Erin, Greta, Annie, Laura, Katharine, Pat, Seth, Jack, Bernadette, Katie, Elise, Lauren, Sarah, Brooke, Katie K., Jen, Handy, Fred, and everyone else, thank you so much.

My family: the Gammills, the Walkers, Granny and Grandma, Amanda, and the Kaplans.

Amherst College, where I went to write some of this book but ended up mostly procrastinating (just like college!). Thank you especially to my amazingly encouraging advisor, Helen Von Schmidt.

Thank you to the staff of *The Daily Show* when I worked there, and the staffs of the various bars and restaurants in New York that I frequent far too often.

Thank you to everyone else who I forgot, who will surely forgive me.

TOW BOOKS

THE TOW BOOKS STORY

BY JOHN WARNER, CHIEF CREATIVE CZAR

On August 18th, 1948, my great uncle, Allan T. Warner (Tow Truck King of Tecumseh Michigan), told a joke to Stanley Johnson as they bumped their way back to the repair shop following Stanley's latest driving mishap. To ease Stanley's upset, Uncle Allan turned to him and said, "Stanley, have you ever heard the one about the horse, the rabbi and the one legged duck who went into a bar…?"

From that day forward, people who needed a tow from Warner Wrecking and Towing were treated to short entertainments, jokes, and yarns, spun by Uncle Allan himself.

To keep people from deliberately crashing their cars just so they could hear the latest hilarious offerings from Uncle Allan, he began collecting them in pamphlets and selling them out of his service station, giving birth to "The Official Warner Books" (TOW Books).

Over the next 25 years TOW Books published 107 volumes. On August 26, 1973, Uncle Allan hung up his winch and released his final title, *A Rabbi, a One-Legged Duck and a Bunch of Dirty Hippies in a Volkswagen Bus With a Busted Distributor Who Don't Have Any Money, But Think It's Okay to Pay Hard Working People in "Good Karma" Walk Into a Bar and Get Their Teeth Kicked In Because They Deserve It.*

We're pleased to renew Uncle Allan's commitment to publishing "funny books for people with good senses of humor."

A VISUAL GUIDE TO YOUR CHILD'S MOODS

It is sometimes hard to know when exactly to engage your child and when to leave them the hell alone already. I have identified every facial expression corresponding to mood that your child could possibly have when they are around you and have labeled them appropriately. By using this simple chart, you can accurately identify your child's mood and proceed thusly.

 HOLIDAY ROAD: They are probably drunk but trying to keep it a secret by screwing up their face in a manner that they, in their drunken state, believe appears natural. This look happens exclusively during the holidays. Avoid them.

 THE WINKY-LOO: Your child is clearly sleep-deprived and a little slaphappy and has decided to wink at you in a saucy manner. They are either hung over or still drunk. Ignore them.

 OPEN-MOUTH SMILE FACE: The open-mouth smile is an unnatural smile characterized by parted mouth and teeth and a frozen smile, as if their mouth were in some sort of apparatus at the dentist's. This means that they have checked out and are thinking about something completely different while they talk to you, probably sex. Do not call them out. In fact, use this opportunity to tell them exactly how you feel. It will filter into their subconscious, but they will not directly process it at the time. This benefits you both.

WORDS AND PHRASES NEVER TO USE

- Erotic
- I created an online profile.
- Insurance (in reference to your child's lack thereof)
- Hook up (I realize you think this means "to get in touch with." You are wrong.)
- Are you smoking the marijuana cigarettes?
- I'm a vegan.

- Old-timey words for "friend" such as: chum, mate.
- I'm staying in your studio apartment with you for the weekend.
- I'm not trying to guilt you into this, I'm just asking you.
- Oriental (Just don't use this word in general.)
- Speculum (If you don't know what this is, look it up.)

INADVERTENTLY SKEPTICAL FACE: It appears as though your child, with one raised eyebrow, is skeptically considering you. However, they are just practicing their one-eyebrow raise, which they have been trying to do since childhood. Now that they can do it, they have to learn how to control it, which is proving exceedingly difficult. Just assume that they are in a normal mood and that you may converse with them in a normal manner. Note: When they actually are skeptical, both eyebrows will rise, like this, so that it looks like they are surprised, but they just cannot control the one eyebrow that they have trained. So, skeptical-seeming face=normal, surprised face=skeptical.

 POLITICALLY INCORRECT OLD-TIMEY REFERENCE FACE: Your child appears to be extremely high on marijuana, which leads you to say, "By Jove, you look like a Chinaman in an opium den!" Leave them be. Also, never say that again. Oh, and Persian rugs are no longer referred to as "Oriental rugs."

 STRUNG OUT-A-GO-GO: Characterized by bloodshot eyes and a puckered mouth the size of a dime, this look corresponds to when your child is determined to get along with you no matter what the cost and keeps their rage bottled up. Don't push it—they could explode at any moment.

WORDS AND PHRASES TO USE

- Here's $1,000.

- Here's another $1,000.

- You're right, it is annoying when I ask you to set the table, and I, too, cannot pinpoint the exact reason why.

- Everyone knows that a six-pack is not enough for you and two friends.

- (Corollary to previous.) Here is some beer money.

- I would never dream of sharing a bed with you in your studio apartment for the weekend.

- You look very thin.

- I don't know how you got to be so much better-looking than me.